Your
Ho[roscope]
2010

♓

Pisces

Your Personal Horoscope 2010

Pisces
20th February–20th March

igloo

igloo

This edition published by Igloo Books Ltd,
Cottage Farm, Sywell, Northants NN6 0BJ
www.igloo-books.com

Produced for Igloo Books by W. Foulsham & Co. Ltd,
The Oriel, Thames Valley Court, 183–187 Bath Road, Slough,
Berkshire SL1 4AA, England

ISBN: 978-1-84817-686-7

Copyright © 2009 W. Foulsham & Co. Ltd

All rights reserved

This is an abridged version of material
originally published in *Old Moore's Horoscope
and Astral Diary*.

The Copyright Act prohibits (subject to certain
very limited exceptions) the making of copies of
any copyright work or of a substantial part of such
a work, including the making of copies by
photocopying or similar process. Written
permission to make a copy or copies must
therefore normally be obtained from the publisher
in advance. It is advisable also to consult the
publisher if in any doubt as to the legality of any
copying which is to be undertaken.

Printed and manufactured in China

CONTENTS

1	Introduction	7
2	The Essence of Pisces: Exploring the Personality of Pisces the Fishes	9
3	Pisces on the Cusp	15
4	Pisces and its Ascendants	17
5	The Moon and the Part it Plays in your Life	31
6	Moon Signs	35
7	Pisces in Love	39
8	Venus: The Planet of Love	43
9	Venus through the Zodiac Signs	45
10	Pisces: 2009 Diary Pages	49
11	Pisces: 2010 Diary Pages	71
12	Pisces: 2010 In Brief	72
13	Rising Signs for Pisces	157
14	The Zodiac, Planets and Correspondences	159

INTRODUCTION

Your Personal Horoscopes have been specifically created to allow you to get the most from astrological patterns and the way they have a bearing on not only your zodiac sign, but nuances within it. Using the diary section of the book you can read about the influences and possibilities of each and every day of the year. It will be possible for you to see when you are likely to be cheerful and happy or those times when your nature is in retreat and you will be more circumspect. The diary will help to give you a feel for the specific 'cycles' of astrology and the way they can subtly change your day-to-day life. For example, when you see the sign ☿, this means that the planet Mercury is retrograde at that time. Retrograde means it appears to be running backwards through the zodiac. Such a happening has a significant effect on communication skills, but this is only one small aspect of how the Personal Horoscope can help you.

With Your Personal Horoscope the story doesn't end with the diary pages. It includes simple ways for you to work out the zodiac sign the Moon occupied at the time of your birth, and what this means for your personality. In addition, if you know the time of day you were born, it is possible to discover your Ascendant, yet another important guide to your personal make-up and potential.

Many readers are interested in relationships and in knowing how well they get on with people of other astrological signs. You might also be interested in the way you appear to very different sorts of individuals. If you are such a person, the section on Venus will be of particular interest. Despite the rapidly changing position of this planet, you can work out your Venus sign, and learn what bearing it will have on your life.

Using Your Personal Horoscope you can travel on one of the most fascinating and rewarding journeys that anyone can take – the journey to a better realisation of self.

THE ESSENCE OF PISCES

Exploring the Personality of Pisces the Fishes

(20TH FEBRUARY– 20TH MARCH)

What's in a sign?

Pisceans are fascinating people – everyone you come across is likely to admit that fact. By nature you are kind, loving, trustful and inclined to work very hard on behalf of the people you love – and perhaps even those you don't like very much. Your nature is sympathetic and you will do anything you can to improve the lot of those you consider to be worse off than yourself. There is a very forgiving side to your temperament and also a strong artistic flair that can find an outlet in any one of a dozen different ways.

It's true you are difficult to know, and there is a very important reason for this. Your nature goes deep, so deep in fact that someone would have to live with you for a lifetime to plumb even a part of its fathomless depths. What the world sees is only ever a small part of the total magic of this most compulsive and fascinating zodiac sign. Much of your latent power and natural magic is constantly kept bottled up, because it is never your desire to manipulate those around you. Rather, you tend to wait in the shadows until opportunities to come into your own present themselves.

In love you are ardent and sincere, though sometimes inclined to choose a partner too readily and too early. There's a dreamy quality to your nature that makes you easy to adore, but which can also cause difficulties if the practical necessities of life take a very definite second place.

The chances are that you love music and picturesque scenery, and you may also exhibit a definite fondness for animals. You prefer to live in the country rather than in the middle of a noisy and smelly town, and tend to keep a reasonably well-ordered household. Your family can easily become your life and you always need a focus for your energies. You are not at all good at feathering your own nest, unless you know that someone else is also going to benefit on the

THE ESSENCE OF PISCES

way. A little more selfishness probably would not go amiss on occasions because you are often far too willing to put yourself out wholesale for people who don't respect your sacrifices. Pisceans can be full of raging passions and are some of the most misunderstood people to be found anywhere within the great circle of the zodiac.

Pisces resources

It is the very essence of your zodiac sign that you are probably sitting there and saying to yourself 'Resources? I have no resources'. Of course you are wrong, though it has to be admitted that a glaring self-confidence isn't likely to be listed amongst them. You are, however, a very deep thinker, and this can turn out to be a great advantage and a useful tool when it comes to getting on in life. Because your natural intuition is so strong (some people would call you psychic), you are rarely fooled by the glib words of others. Your own natural tendency to tell the truth can be a distinct advantage and a great help to you when it comes to getting on in life from a practical and financial viewpoint.

Whilst many of the signs of the zodiac tend to respond to life in an impulsive way, you are more likely to weigh up the pros and cons of any given situation very carefully. This means that when you do take action you can achieve much more success – as well as saving a good deal of energy on the way. People tend to confide in you automatically, so you are definitely at an advantage when it comes to knowing what makes your family and friends tick. At work you can labour quietly and confidently, either on your own or in the company of others. Some people would assert that Pisceans are model employees because you really do not know how to give anything less than your best.

Never underestimate the power of your instincts. Under most circumstances you are aware of the possible outcome of any given situation and should react as your inner mind dictates. Following this course inevitably puts you ahead of the game and explains why so quiet a sign can promote so many winners in life. Not that you are particularly competitive. It's much more important for you to be part of a winning team than to be out there collecting the glory for yourself.

You are dependable, kind, loving and peerless in your defence of those you take to. All of these are incredible resources when used in the correct way. Perhaps most important of all is your ability to get others on your side. In this you cannot be matched.

Beneath the surface

Everyone instinctively knows that there is something very important going on beneath the surface of the Piscean mind, though working out exactly what it might be is a different kettle of fish altogether. The fact is that you are very secretive about yourself and tend to give very little away. There are occasions when this tendency can be a saving grace, but others where it is definitely a great disadvantage. What isn't hard to see is your natural sympathy and your desire to help those in trouble. There's no end gain here, it's simply the way you are. Your inspiration to do anything is rarely rooted in what your own prize is likely to be. In your soul you are poetical, deeply romantic and inextricably tied to the forces and cycles of the world that brought you to birth.

Despite your capacity for single-minded concentration in some matters, you are often subject to mental confusion. Rational considerations often take second place to intuitive foresight and even inspiration. Making leaps in logic isn't at all unusual for you and forms part of the way you judge the world and deal with it.

If you really want to get on in life, and to gain the most you can from your interactions with others, you need to be very truthful in your approach. Somehow or other that means finding out what is really going on in your mind and explaining it to those around you. This is never going to be an easy process, partly because of your naturally secretive ways. Actually some astrologers overplay the tendency of Pisces to keep its secrets. A great deal of the time you simply don't think you have anything to say that would interest others and you always lack confidence in your own judgements. This is a shame because you rarely proceed without thinking carefully and don't often make glaring mistakes.

Many Pisceans develop an ingrained tendency to believe themselves inadequate in some way. Once again this is something you should fight against. Knowing others better, and allowing them to get to know you, might cause you to feel less quirky or strange. Whether you realise it or not you have a natural magnetism that draws others towards you. Try to spend rather less time thinking – though without losing that Piscean ability to meditate which is central to your well-being. If you allow the fascinating world of the Piscean mind to be shared by the people you come to trust, you should become more understandable to people who really want to like you even more.

Making the best of yourself

It must be remembered that the zodiac sign of Pisces represents two Fishes, tethered by a cord but constantly trying to break away from each other. This says a great deal about the basic Piscean nature. The inward, contemplative side of your personality is often at odds with the more gregarious and chatty qualities you also possess. Learning about this duality of nature can go at least part of the way towards dealing with it.

Although you often exhibit a distinct lack of self-confidence in your dealings with the world at large, you are, at heart, quite adept, flexible and able to cope under almost any circumstance. All that is really required in order to have a positive influence on life and to be successful is for you to realise what you are capable of achieving. Alas this isn't quite as easy as it might appear, because the introspective depths of your nature make you think too much and cause you to avoid the very actions that would get you noticed more. This can be something of a dilemma for Pisces, though it is certainly not insurmountable.

Never be afraid to allow your sensitivity to show. It is one of your greatest assets and it is part of the reason why other people love you so much – far more, in fact, than you probably realise. Your natural warmth, grace and charm are certain to turn heads on those occasions when you can't avoid being watched. The creative qualities that you possess make it possible for you to manufacture harmonious surroundings, both for yourself and for your family, who are very important to you. At the same time you recognise the practical in life and don't mind getting your hands dirty, especially when it comes to helping someone else out of a mess.

One of the best ruses Pisceans can use in order to get over the innate shyness that often attends the sign is to put on an act. Pisceans are very good natural actors and can easily assume the role of another individual. So, in your dealings with the world at large, manufacture a more confident individual, though without leaving out all the wonderful things that make you what you are now. Play this part for all you are worth and you will then truly be making the best of yourself.

The impressions you give

There is absolutely no doubt that you are more popular, admired and even fancied than you could ever believe. Such is the natural modesty of your zodiac sign that you invariably fail to pick up on those little messages coming across from other people that say 'I think you are wonderful'. If we don't believe in ourselves it's difficult for us to accept that others think we are worth their consideration. Failing to realise your worth to the world at large is likely to be your greatest fault and needs to be corrected.

In a way it doesn't matter, when seen from the perspective of others. What they observe is a warm-hearted individual. Your magnetic personality is always on display, whether you intend it to be or not, which is another reason why you tend to attract far more attention than you would sometimes elicit. Most Pisceans are quite sexy, another quality that is bound to come across to the people you meet, at least some of whom would be willing to jump through hoops if you were to command it.

In short, what you show, and what you think you are, could be two entirely different things. If you don't believe this to be the case you need to carry out a straw poll amongst some of the people you know. Ask them to write down all your qualities as they see them. The result will almost certainly surprise you and demonstrate that you are far more capable, and loveable, than you believe yourself to be. Armed with this knowledge you can walk forward in life with more confidence and feel as content inside as you appear to be when viewed by the world at large.

People rely heavily on you. That much at least you will have noticed in a day-to-day sense. They do so because they know how well you deal with almost any situation. Even in a crisis you show your true colours and that's part of the reason why so many Piscean people find themselves involved in the medical profession. You are viewed as being stronger than you believe yourself to be, which is why everyone tends to be so surprised when they discover that you are vulnerable and inclined to worry.

The way forward

You have a great deal to offer the world, even if you don't always appreciate how much. Although you are capable of being shy and introverted on occasions, you are equally likely to be friendly, chatty and very co-operative. You settle to just about any task, though you do possess a sense of freedom that makes it difficult for you to be cooped up in the same place for days and weeks at a stretch. You prefer the sort of tasks that allow your own natural proclivities to shine out, and you exhibit an instinctive creative tendency in almost anything you do.

Use your natural popularity to the full. People are always willing to put themselves out on your behalf, mainly because they know how generous you are and want to repay you for some previous favour. You should never be too proud to accept this sort of proffered help and must avoid running away with the idea that you are unequal to any reasonable task that you set yourself.

It's true that some of your thoughts are extremely deep and that you can get yourself into something of a brown study on occasions, which can be translated by the world around you as depression. However, you are far more stable than you probably believe yourself to be because Pisces is actually one of the toughest of the zodiac signs.

Because you are born of a Water sign it is likely that you would take great delight in living near the sea, or some other large body of water. This isn't essential to your well-being but it does feed your imagination. The vastness of nature in all its forms probably appeals to you in any case and most Pisceans love the natural world with its staggering diversity.

In love you are ardent and sincere, but you do need to make sure that you choose the right individual to suit you. Pisceans often settle for a protecting arm, but if this turns out to be stifling, trouble could follow. You would find it hard to live with anyone who didn't have at least a degree of your sensitivity, and you need a partner who will allow you to retain that sense of inner freedom that is so vital to your well-being.

Make the most of the many gifts and virtues that nature has bestowed upon you and don't be afraid to let people know what you really are. Actually establishing this in the first place isn't easy for you. Pisceans respond well to almost any form of meditation, which is not surprising because the sign of the Fishes is the most spiritually motivated zodiac sign of them all. When you know yourself fully you generate a personality that is an inspiration to everyone.

PISCES ON THE CUSP

Astrological profiles are altered for those people born at either the beginning or the end of a zodiac sign, or, more properly, on the cusps of a sign. In the case of Pisces this would be on the 20th of February and for two or three days after, and similarly at the end of the sign, probably from the 18th to the 20th of March.

The Aquarius Cusp – February 20th to 22nd

This tends to be a generally happy combination of signs, even if some of the people you come into contact with find you rather difficult to understand from time to time. You are quite capable of cutting a dash, as any Aquarian would be, and yet at the same time you have the quiet and contemplative qualities more typified by Pisces. You tend to be seen as an immensely attractive person, even if you are the last one in the world to accept this fact. People find you to be friendly, very approachable and good company in almost any social or personal setting. It isn't hard for you to get on with others, though since you are not so naturally quiet as Pisces when taken alone, you are slightly more willing to speak your mind and to help out, though usually in a very diplomatic manner.

At work you are very capable and many people with this combination find themselves working on behalf of humanity as a whole. Thus work in social services, hospitals or charities really suits the unique combinations thrown up by this sign mixture. Management is right up your street, though there are times when your conception of popularity takes the foremost place in your mind. Occasionally this could take the edge off executive decisions. A careful attention to detail shows you in a position to get things done, even jobs that others shun. You don't really care for getting your hands dirty but will tackle almost any task if you know it to be necessary. Being basically self-sufficient, you also love the company of others, and it is this adaptability that is the hallmark of success to Aquarian-cusp Pisceans.

Few people actually know you as well as they think they do because the waters of your nature run quite deep. Your real task in life is to let the world know how you feel, something you fight shy of doing now and again. There are positive gains in your life, brought about as a result of your adaptable and pleasing nature. Aquarius present in the nature allows Pisces to act at its best.

The Aries Cusp – March 18th to 20th

This is a Piscean with attitude and probably one of the most difficult zodiac sign combinations to be understood, not only by those people with whom you come into contact but clearly by yourself too. If there are any problems thrown up here they come from the fact that Pisces and Aries have such different ways of expressing themselves to the world at large. Aries is very upfront, dynamic and dominant, all factors that are simply diametrically opposed to the way Pisces thinks and behaves. So the real task in life is to find ways to combine the qualities of Pisces and Aries, in a way that suits the needs of both and without becoming totally confused with regard to your basic nature.

The problem is usually solved by a compartmentation of life. For example, many people with this combination will show the Aries qualities strongly at work, whilst dropping into the Piscean mode socially and at home. This may invariably be the case but there are bound to be times when the underlying motivations become mixed, which can confuse those with whom you come into contact.

Having said all of this you can be the least selfish and most successful individual when you are fighting for the rights of others. This is the zodiac combination of the true social reformer, the genuine politician and the committed pacifist. It seems paradoxical to suggest that someone could fight tenaciously for peace, but this is certainly true in your case. You have excellent executive skills and yet retain an ability to tell other people what they should be doing, in fairly strident terms, usually without upsetting anyone. There is a degree of genuine magic about you that makes you very attractive and there is likely to be more than one love affair in your life. A steadfast view of romance may not be naturally present within your basic nature but like so much else you can 'train' this quality into existence.

Personal success is likely, but it probably doesn't matter all that much in a material sense. The important thing to you is being needed by the world at large.

PISCES AND ITS ASCENDANTS

The nature of every individual on the planet is composed of the rich variety of zodiac signs and planetary positions that were present at the time of their birth. Your Sun sign, which in your case is Pisces, is one of the many factors when it comes to assessing the unique person you are. Probably the most important consideration, other than your Sun sign, is to establish the zodiac sign that was rising over the eastern horizon at the time that you were born. This is your Ascending or Rising sign. Most popular astrology fails to take account of the Ascendant, and yet its importance remains with you from the very moment of your birth, through every day of your life. The Ascendant is evident in the way you approach the world, and so, when meeting a person for the first time, it is this astrological influence that you are most likely to notice first. Our Ascending sign essentially represents what we appear to be, while the Sun sign is what we feel inside ourselves.

The Ascendant also has the potential for modifying our overall nature. For example, if you were born at a time of day when Pisces was passing over the eastern horizon (this would be around the time of dawn) then you would be classed as a double Pisces. As such, you would typify this zodiac sign, both internally and in your dealings with others. However, if your Ascendant sign turned out to be a Fire sign, such as Aries, there would be a profound alteration of nature, away from the expected qualities of Pisces.

One of the reasons why popular astrology often ignores the Ascendant is that it has always been rather difficult to establish. We have found a way to make this possible by devising an easy-to-use table, which you will find on page 157 of this book. Using this, you can establish your Ascendant sign at a glance. You will need to know your rough time of birth, then it is simply a case of following the instructions.

For those readers who have no idea of their time of birth it might be worth allowing a good friend, or perhaps your partner, to read through the section that follows this introduction. Someone who deals with you on a regular basis may easily discover your Ascending sign, even though you could have some difficulty establishing it for yourself. A good understanding of this component of your nature is essential if you want to be aware of that 'other person' who is responsible for the way you make contact with the world at large. Your Sun sign, Ascendant sign, and the other pointers in this book will, together, allow you a far better understanding of what makes you tick as an individual. Peeling back the different layers of your astrological make-up can be an enlightening experience, and the Ascendant may represent one of the most important layers of all.

Pisces with Pisces Ascendant

You are a kind and considerate person who would do almost anything to please the people around you. Creative and extremely perceptive, nobody knows the twists and turns of human nature better than you do, and you make it your business to serve humanity in any way you can. Not everyone understands what makes you tick, and part of the reason for this state of affairs is that you are often not really quite 'in' the world as much as the people you encounter in a day-to-day sense. At work you are generally cheerful, though you can be very quiet on occasions, but since you are consistent in this regard, you don't attract adverse attention or accusations of being moody, as some other variants of Pisces sometimes do. Confusion can beset you on occasions, especially when you are trying to reconcile your own opposing needs. There are certain moments of discontent to be encountered which so often come from trying to please others, even when to do so goes against your own instincts.

As age and experience add to your personal armoury you relax more with the world and find yourself constantly sought out for words of wisdom. The vast majority of people care for you deeply.

Pisces with Aries Ascendant

Although not an easy combination to deal with, the Pisces with an Aries Ascendant does bring something very special to the world in the way of natural understanding allied to practical assistance. It's true that you can sometimes be a dreamer, but there is nothing wrong with that as long as you have the ability to turn some of your wishes into reality, and this you are usually able to do, often for the sake of those around you. Conversation comes easily to you, though you also possess a slightly wistful and poetic side to your nature, which is attractive to the many people who call you a friend. A natural entertainer, you bring a sense of the comic to the often serious qualities of Aries, though without losing the determination that typifies the sign.

In relationships you are ardent, sincere and supportive, with a social conscience that sometimes finds you fighting the battles of the less privileged members of society. Family is important to you and this is a combination that invariably leads to parenthood. Away from the cut and thrust of everyday life you relax more fully, and think about matters more deeply than more typical Aries types might.

Pisces with Taurus Ascendant

You are clearly a very sensitive type of person and that sometimes makes it rather difficult for others to know how they might best approach you. Private and deep, you are nevertheless socially inclined on many occasions. However, because your nature is bottomless it is possible that some types would actually accuse you of being shallow. How can this come about? Well, it's simple really. The fact is that you rarely show anyone what is going on in the deepest recesses of your mind and so your responses can appear to be trite or even ill-considered. This is far from the truth, as those who are allowed into the 'inner sanctum' would readily admit. You are something of a sensualist, and relish staying in bed late and simply pleasing yourself for days on end. However, you have Taurean traits so you desire a tidy environment in which to live your usually long life.

You are able to deal with the routine aspects of life quite well and can be a capable worker once you are up and firing on all cylinders. It is very important that you maintain an interest in what you are doing, because the recesses of your dreamy mind can sometimes appear to be infinitely more attractive. Your imagination is second to none and this fact can often be turned to your advantage.

Pisces with Gemini Ascendant

There is great duality inherent in this combination, and sometimes this can cause a few problems. Part of the trouble stems from the fact that you often fail to realise what you want from life, and you could also be accused of failing to take the time out to think things through carefully enough. You are reactive, and although you have every bit of the natural charm that typifies the sign of Gemini, you are more prone to periods of self-doubt and confusion. However, you should not allow these facts to get you down too much, because you are also genuinely loved and have a tremendous capacity to look after others, a factor which is more important to you than any other. It's true that personal relationships can sometimes be a cause of difficulty for you, partly because your constant need to know what makes other people tick could drive them up the wall. Accepting people at face value seems to be the best key to happiness of a personal sort, and there are occasions when your very real and natural intuition has to be put on hold.

It's likely that you are an original, particularly in the way you dress. An early rebellious stage often gives way to a more comfortable form of eccentricity. When you are at your best, just about everyone adores you.

Pisces with Cancer Ascendant

A deep, double Water-sign combination this, and it might serve to make you a very misunderstood, though undoubtedly popular, individual. You are anxious to make a good impression, probably too keen under certain circumstances, and you do everything you can to help others, even if you don't know them very well. It's true that you are deeply sensitive and quite easily brought to tears by the suffering of this most imperfect world that we inhabit. Fatigue can be a problem, though this is somewhat nullified by the fact that you can withdraw completely into the deep recesses of your own mind when it becomes necessary to do so.

You may not be the most gregarious person in the world, simply because it isn't easy for you to put some of your most important considerations into words. This is easier when you are in the company of people you know and trust, though even trust is a commodity that is difficult for you to find, particularly since you may have been hurt by being too willing to share your thoughts early in life. With age comes wisdom and maturity, and the older you are, the better you will learn to handle this potent and demanding combination. You will never go short of either friends or would-be lovers, and may be one of the most magnetic types of both Cancer and Pisces.

Pisces with Leo Ascendant

You are a very sensitive soul, on occasions too much so for your own good. However, there is not a better advocate for the rights of humanity than you represent and you constantly do what you can to support the downtrodden and oppressed. Good causes are your thing and there are likely to be many in your life. You will probably find yourself pushed to the front of almost any enterprise of which you are a part because, despite the deeper qualities of Pisces, you are a natural leader. Even on those occasions when it feels as though you lack confidence, you manage to muddle through somehow and your smile is as broad as the day. Few sign combinations are more loved than this one, mainly because you do not have a malicious bone in your body, and will readily forgive and forget, which the Lion on its own often will not.

Although you are capable of acting on impulse, you do so from a deep sense of moral conviction, so that most of your endeavours are designed to suit other people too. They recognise this fact and will push much support back in your direction. Even when you come across troubles in your life you manage to find ways to sort them out, and will invariably notice something new to smile about on the way. Your sensitivity rating is massive and you can easily be moved to tears.

Pisces with Virgo Ascendant

You might have been accused on occasions of being too sensitive for your own good, a charge that is not entirely without foundation. Certainly you are very understanding of the needs of others, sometimes to the extent that you put everything aside to help them. This would also be true in the case of charities, for you care very much about the world and the people who cling tenaciously to its surface. Your ability to love on a one-to-one basis knows no bounds, though you may not discriminate as much as you could, particularly when young, and might have one or two false starts in the love stakes. You don't always choose to verbalise your thoughts and this can cause problems, because there is always so much going on in your mind and Virgo especially needs good powers of communication. Pisces is quieter and you need to force yourself to say what you think when the explanation is important.

You would never betray a confidence and sometimes take on rather more for the sake of your friends than is strictly good for you. This is not a fault but can cause you problems all the same. Because you are so intuitive there is little that escapes your attention, though you should avoid being pessimistic about your insights. Changes of scenery suit you and travel would bring out the best in what can be a repressed nature.

Pisces with Libra Ascendant

An Air and Water combination, you are not easy to understand and have depths that show at times, surprising those people who thought they already knew what you were. You will always keep people guessing and are just as likely to hitchhike around Europe as you are to hold down a steady job, both of which you would undertake with the same degree of commitment and success. Usually young at heart, but always carrying the potential for an old head on young shoulders, you are something of a paradox and not at all easy for totally 'straight' types to understand. But you always make an impression, and tend to be very attractive to members of the opposite sex.

In matters of health you do have to be a little careful because you dissipate much nervous energy and can sometimes be inclined to push yourself too hard, at least in a mental sense. Frequent periods of rest and meditation will do you the world of good and should improve your level of wisdom, which tends to be fairly high already. Much of your effort in life is expounded on behalf of humanity as a whole, for you care deeply, love totally and always give of your best. Whatever your faults and failings might be, you are one of the most popular people around.

Pisces with Scorpio Ascendant

You stand a chance of disappearing so deep into yourself that other people would need one of those long ladders that cave explorers use to even find you. It isn't really your fault, because both Scorpio and Pisces, as Water signs, are difficult to understand and you have them both. But that doesn't mean that you should be content to remain in the dark, and the warmth of your nature is all you need to shine a light on the wonderful qualities you possess. But the primary word of warning is that you must put yourself on display and allow others to know what you are, before their appreciation of these facts becomes apparent.

As a server of the world you are second to none and it is hard to find a person with this combination who is not, in some way, looking out for the people around them. Immensely attractive to others, you are also one of the most sought-after lovers. Much of this has to do with your deep and abiding charm, but the air of mystery that surrounds you also helps. Some of you will marry too early, and end up regretting the fact, though the majority of people with Scorpio and Pisces will find the love they deserve in the end. You are able, just, firm but fair, though a sucker for a hard luck story and as kind as the day is long. It's hard to imagine how so many good points could be ignored by others.

Pisces with Sagittarius Ascendant

A very attractive combination this, because the more dominant qualities of the Archer are somehow mellowed-out by the caring Water-sign qualities of the Fishes. You can be very outgoing, but there is always a deeper side to your nature that allows others to know that you are thinking about them. Few people could fall out with either your basic nature or your attitude to the world at large, even though there are depths to your nature that may not be easily understood. You are capable, have a good executive ability and can work hard to achieve your objectives, even if you get a little disillusioned on the way. Much of your life is given over to helping those around you and there is a great tendency for you to work for and on behalf of humanity as a whole. A sense of community is brought to most of what you do and you enjoy co-operation. Although you have the natural ability to attract people to you, the Pisces half of your nature makes you just a little more reserved in personal matters than might otherwise be the case. More careful in your choices than either sign taken alone, you still have to make certain that your motivations when commencing a personal relationship are the right ones. You love to be happy, and to offer gifts of happiness to others.

Pisces with Capricorn Ascendant

You are certainly not the easiest person in the world to understand, mainly because your nature is so deep and your personality so complicated, that others are somewhat intimidated at the prospect of staring into this abyss. All the same your friendly nature is attractive, and there will always be people around who are fascinated by the sheer magnetic quality that is intrinsic to this zodiac mix. Sentimental and extremely kind, there is no limit to the extent of your efforts on behalf of a deserving world, though there are some people around who wonder at your commitment and who may ridicule you a little for your staying-power, even in the face of some adversity. At work you are very capable, will work long and hard, and can definitely expect a greater degree of financial and practical success than Pisces when taken alone. Routines don't bother you too much, though you do need regular periods of introspection, which help to recharge low batteries and a battered self-esteem. In affairs of the heart you are given to impulse, which belies the more careful qualities of Capricorn. However, the determination remains intact and you are quite capable of chasing rainbows round and round the same field, never realising that you can't get to the end of them. Generally speaking you are an immensely lovable person and a great favourite to many.

Pisces with Aquarius Ascendant

Here we find the originality of Aquarius balanced by the very sensitive qualities of Pisces, and it makes for a very interesting combination. When it comes to understanding other people you are second to none, but it's certain that you are more instinctive than either Pisces or Aquarius when taken alone. You are better at routines than Aquarius, but also relish a challenge more than the typical Piscean would. Active and enterprising, you tend to know what you want from life, but consideration of others, and the world at large, will always be part of the scenario. People with this combination often work on behalf of humanity and are to be found in social work, the medical profession and religious institutions. As far as beliefs are concerned you don't conform to established patterns, and yet may get closer to the truth of the Creator than many deep theological thinkers have ever been able to do. Acting on impulse as much as you do means that not everyone understands the way your mind works, but your popularity will invariably see you through.

Passionate and deeply sensitive, you are able to negotiate the twists and turns of a romantic life that is hardly likely to be run-of-the-mill. In the end, however, you should certainly be able to find a very deep personal and spiritual happiness.

THE MOON AND THE PART IT PLAYS IN YOUR LIFE

In astrology the Moon is probably the single most important heavenly body after the Sun. Its unique position, as partner to the Earth on its journey around the solar system, means that the Moon appears to pass through the signs of the zodiac extremely quickly. The zodiac position of the Moon at the time of your birth plays a great part in personal character and is especially significant in the build-up of your emotional nature.

Your Own Moon Sign

Discovering the position of the Moon at the time of your birth has always been notoriously difficult because tracking the complex zodiac positions of the Moon is not easy. This process has been reduced to three simple stages with our Lunar Tables. A breakdown of the Moon's zodiac positions can be found from page 35 onwards, so that once you know what your Moon Sign is, you can see what part this plays in the overall build-up of your personal character.

If you follow the instructions on the next page you will soon be able to work out exactly what zodiac sign the Moon occupied on the day that you were born and you can then go on to compare the reading for this position with those of your Sun sign and your Ascendant. It is partly the comparison between these three important positions that goes towards making you the unique individual you are.

THE MOON IN YOUR LIFE

HOW TO DISCOVER YOUR MOON SIGN

This is a three-stage process. You may need a pen and a piece of paper but if you follow the instructions below the process should only take a minute or so.

STAGE 1 First of all you need to know the Moon Age at the time of your birth. If you look at Moon Table 1, on page 33, you will find all the years between 1912 and 2010 down the left side. Find the year of your birth and then trace across to the right to the month of your birth. Where the two intersect you will find a number. This is the date of the New Moon in the month that you were born. You now need to count forward the number of days between the New Moon and your own birthday. For example, if the New Moon in the month of your birth was shown as being the 6th and you were born on the 20th, your Moon Age Day would be 14. If the New Moon in the month of your birth came after your birthday, you need to count forward from the New Moon in the previous month. If you were born in a Leap Year, remember to count the 29th February. You can tell if your birth year was a Leap Year if the last two digits can be divided by four. Whatever the result, jot this number down so that you do not forget it.

STAGE 2 Take a look at Moon Table 2 on page 34. Down the left hand column look for the date of your birth. Now trace across to the month of your birth. Where the two meet you will find a letter. Copy this letter down alongside your Moon Age Day.

STAGE 3 Moon Table 3 on page 34 will supply you with the zodiac sign the Moon occupied on the day of your birth. Look for your Moon Age Day down the left hand column and then for the letter you found in Stage 2. Where the two converge you will find a zodiac sign and this is the sign occupied by the Moon on the day that you were born.

Your Zodiac Moon Sign Explained

You will find a profile of all zodiac Moon Signs on pages 35 to 38, showing in yet another way how astrology helps to make you into the individual that you are. In each daily entry of the Astral Diary you can find the zodiac position of the Moon for every day of the year. This also allows you to discover your lunar birthdays. Since the Moon passes through all the signs of the zodiac in about a month, you can expect something like twelve lunar birthdays each year. At these times you are likely to be emotionally steady and able to make the sort of decisions that have real, lasting value.

MOON TABLE 1

YEAR	JAN	FEB	MAR	YEAR	JAN	FEB	MAR	YEAR	JAN	FEB	MAR
1912	18	17	19	1945	14	12	14	1978	9	7	9
1913	7	6	7	1946	3	2	3	1979	27	26	27
1914	25	24	26	1947	21	19	21	1980	16	15	16
1915	15	15	14	1948	11	9	11	1981	6	4	6
1916	5	3	5	1949	29	27	29	1982	25	23	24
1917	24	22	23	1950	18	16	18	1983	14	13	14
1918	12	11	12	1951	7	6	7	1984	3	1	2
1919	1/31	–	2/31	1952	26	25	25	1985	21	19	21
1920	21	19	20	1953	15	14	15	1986	10	9	10
1921	9	8	9	1954	5	3	5	1987	29	28	29
1922	27	26	28	1955	24	22	24	1988	18	17	18
1923	17	15	17	1956	13	11	12	1989	7	6	7
1924	6	5	5	1957	1/30	–	1/31	1990	26	25	26
1925	24	23	24	1958	19	18	20	1991	15	14	15
1926	14	12	14	1959	9	7	9	1992	4	3	4
1927	3	2	3	1960	27	26	27	1993	24	22	24
1928	21	19	21	1961	16	15	16	1994	11	10	12
1929	11	9	11	1962	6	5	6	1995	1/31	29	30
1930	29	28	30	1963	25	23	25	1996	19	18	19
1931	18	17	19	1964	14	13	14	1997	9	7	9
1932	7	6	7	1965	3	1	2	1998	27	26	27
1933	25	24	26	1966	21	19	21	1999	16	15	16
1934	15	14	15	1967	10	9	10	2000	6	4	6
1935	5	3	5	1968	29	28	29	2001	24	23	25
1936	24	22	23	1969	19	17	18	2002	13	12	13
1937	12	11	12	1970	7	6	7	2003	3	1	2
1938	1/31	–	2/31	1971	26	25	26	2004	21	20	21
1939	20	19	20	1972	15	14	15	2005	10	9	10
1940	9	8	9	1973	5	4	5	2006	29	28	29
1941	27	26	27	1974	24	22	24	2007	18	16	18
1942	16	15	16	1975	12	11	12	2008	8	6	7
1943	6	4	6	1976	1/31	29	30	2009	26	25	26
1944	25	24	24	1977	19	18	19	2010	15	14	15

THE MOON IN YOUR LIFE

TABLE 2

DAY	FEB	MAR
1	D	F
2	D	G
3	D	G
4	D	G
5	D	G
6	D	G
7	D	G
8	D	G
9	D	G
10	E	G
11	E	G
12	E	H
13	E	H
14	E	H
15	E	H
16	E	H
17	E	H
18	E	H
19	E	H
20	F	H
21	F	H
22	F	I
23	F	I
24	F	I
25	F	I
26	F	I
27	F	I
28	F	I
29	F	I
30	–	I
31	–	I

MOON TABLE 3

M/D	D	E	F	G	H	I	J
0	AQ	PI	PI	PI	AR	AR	AR
1	PI	PI	PI	AR	AR	AR	TA
2	PI	PI	AR	AR	AR	TA	TA
3	PI	AR	AR	AR	TA	TA	TA
4	AR	AR	AR	TA	TA	GE	GE
5	AR	TA	TA	TA	GE	GE	GE
6	TA	TA	TA	GE	GE	GE	CA
7	TA	TA	GE	GE	GE	CA	CA
8	TA	GE	GE	GE	CA	CA	CA
9	GE	GE	CA	CA	CA	CA	LE
10	GE	CA	CA	CA	LE	LE	LE
11	CA	CA	CA	LE	LE	LE	VI
12	CA	CA	LE	LE	LE	VI	VI
13	LE	LE	LE	LE	VI	VI	VI
14	LE	LE	VI	VI	VI	LI	LI
15	LE	VI	VI	VI	LI	LI	LI
16	VI	VI	VI	LI	LI	LI	SC
17	VI	VI	LI	LI	LI	SC	SC
18	VI	LI	LI	LI	SC	SC	SC
19	LI	LI	LI	SC	SC	SC	SA
20	LI	SC	SC	SC	SA	SA	SA
21	SC	SC	SC	SA	SA	SA	CP
22	SC	SC	SA	SA	SA	CP	CP
23	SC	SA	SA	SA	CP	CP	CP
24	SA	SA	SA	CP	CP	CP	AQ
25	SA	CP	CP	CP	AQ	AQ	AQ
26	CP	CP	CP	AQ	AQ	AQ	PI
27	CP	AQ	AQ	AQ	AQ	PI	PI
28	AQ	AQ	AQ	AQ	PI	PI	PI
29	AQ	AQ	AQ	PI	PI	PI	AR

AR = Aries, TA = Taurus, GE = Gemini, CA = Cancer, LE = Leo, VI = Virgo, LI = Libra, SC = Scorpio, SA = Sagittarius, CP = Capricorn, AQ = Aquarius, PI = Pisces

MOON SIGNS

Moon in Aries

You have a strong imagination, courage, determination and a desire to do things in your own way and forge your own path through life.

Originality is a key attribute; you are seldom stuck for ideas although your mind is changeable and you could take the time to focus on individual tasks. Often quick-tempered, you take orders from few people and live life at a fast pace. Avoid health problems by taking regular time out for rest and relaxation.

Emotionally, it is important that you talk to those you are closest to and work out your true feelings. Once you discover that people are there to help, there is less necessity for you to do everything yourself.

Moon in Taurus

The Moon in Taurus gives you a courteous and friendly manner, which means you are likely to have many friends.

The good things in life mean a lot to you, as Taurus is an Earth sign that delights in experiences which please the senses. Hence you are probably a lover of good food and drink, which may in turn mean you need to keep an eye on the bathroom scales, especially as looking good is also important to you.

Emotionally you are fairly stable and you stick by your own standards. Taureans do not respond well to change. Intuition also plays an important part in your life.

Moon in Gemini

You have a warm-hearted character, sympathetic and eager to help others. At times reserved, you can also be articulate and chatty: this is part of the paradox of Gemini, which always brings duplicity to the nature. You are interested in current affairs, have a good intellect, and are good company and likely to have many friends. Most of your friends have a high opinion of you and would be ready to defend you should the need arise. However, this is usually unnecessary, as you are quite capable of defending yourself in any verbal confrontation.

Travel is important to your inquisitive mind and you find intellectual stimulus in mixing with people from different cultures. You also gain much from reading, writing and the arts but you do need plenty of rest and relaxation in order to avoid fatigue.

Moon in Cancer

The Moon in Cancer at the time of birth is a fortunate position as Cancer is the Moon's natural home. This means that the qualities of compassion and understanding given by the Moon are especially enhanced in your nature, and you are friendly and sociable and cope well with emotional pressures. You cherish home and family life, and happily do the domestic tasks. Your surroundings are important to you and you hate squalor and filth. You are likely to have a love of music and poetry.

Your basic character, although at times changeable like the Moon itself, depends on symmetry. You aim to make your surroundings comfortable and harmonious, for yourself and those close to you.

Moon in Leo

The best qualities of the Moon and Leo come together to make you warm-hearted, fair, ambitious and self-confident. With good organisational abilities, you invariably rise to a position of responsibility in your chosen career. This is fortunate as you don't enjoy being an 'also-ran' and would rather be an important part of a small organisation than a menial in a large one.

You should be lucky in love, and happy, provided you put in the effort to make a comfortable home for yourself and those close to you. It is likely that you will have a love of pleasure, sport, music and literature. Life brings you many rewards, most of them as a direct result of your own efforts, although you may be luckier than average and ready to make the best of any situation.

Moon in Virgo

You are endowed with good mental abilities and a keen receptive memory, but you are never ostentatious or pretentious. Naturally quite reserved, you still have many friends, especially of the opposite sex. Marital relationships must be discussed carefully and worked at so that they remain harmonious, as personal attachments can be a problem if you do not give them your full attention.

Talented and persevering, you possess artistic qualities and are a good homemaker. Earning your honours through genuine merit, you work long and hard towards your objectives but show little pride in your achievements. Many short journeys will be undertaken in your life.

Moon in Libra

With the Moon in Libra you are naturally popular and make friends easily. People like you, probably more than you realise, you bring fun to a party and are a natural diplomat. For all its good points, Libra is not the most stable of astrological signs and, as a result, your emotions can be a little unstable too. Therefore, although the Moon in Libra is said to be good for love and marriage, your Sun sign and Rising sign will have an important effect on your emotional and loving qualities.

You must remember to relate to others in your decision-making. Co-operation is crucial because Libra represents the 'balance' of life that can only be achieved through harmonious relationships. Conformity is not easy for you because Libra, an Air sign, likes its independence.

Moon in Scorpio

Some people might call you pushy. In fact, all you really want to do is to live life to the full and protect yourself and your family from the pressures of life. Take care to avoid giving the impression of being sarcastic or impulsive and use your energies wisely and constructively.

You have great courage and you invariably achieve your goals by force of personality and sheer effort. You are fond of mystery and are good at predicting the outcome of situations and events. Travel experiences can be beneficial to you.

You may experience problems if you do not take time to examine your motives in a relationship, and also if you allow jealousy, always a feature of Scorpio, to cloud your judgement.

Moon in Sagittarius

The Moon in Sagittarius helps to make you a generous individual with humanitarian qualities and a kind heart. Restlessness may be intrinsic as your mind is seldom still. Perhaps because of this, you have a need for change that could lead you to several major moves during your adult life. You are not afraid to stand your ground when you know your judgement is right, you speak directly and have good intuition.

At work you are quick, efficient and versatile and so you make an ideal employee. You need work to be intellectually demanding and do not enjoy tedious routines.

In relationships, you anger quickly if faced with stupidity or deception, though you are just as quick to forgive and forget. Emotionally, there are times when your heart rules your head.

Moon in Capricorn

The Moon in Capricorn makes you popular and likely to come into the public eye in some way. The watery Moon is not entirely comfortable in the Earth sign of Capricorn and this may lead to some difficulties in the early years of life. An initial lack of creative ability and indecision must be overcome before the true qualities of patience and perseverance inherent in Capricorn can show through.

You have good administrative ability and are a capable worker, and if you are careful you can accumulate wealth. But you must be cautious and take professional advice in partnerships, as you are open to deception. You may be interested in social or welfare work, which suit your organisational skills and sympathy for others.

Moon in Aquarius

The Moon in Aquarius makes you an active and agreeable person with a friendly, easy-going nature. Sympathetic to the needs of others, you flourish in a laid-back atmosphere. You are broad-minded, fair and open to suggestion, although sometimes you have an unconventional quality which others can find hard to understand.

You are interested in the strange and curious, and in old articles and places. You enjoy trips to these places and gain much from them. Political, scientific and educational work interests you and you might choose a career in science or technology.

Money-wise, you make gains through innovation and concentration and Lunar Aquarians often tackle more than one job at a time. In love you are kind and honest.

Moon in Pisces

You have a kind, sympathetic nature, somewhat retiring at times, but you always take account of others' feelings and help when you can.

Personal relationships may be problematic, but as life goes on you can learn from your experiences and develop a better understanding of yourself and the world around you.

You have a fondness for travel, appreciate beauty and harmony and hate disorder and strife. You may be fond of literature and would make a good writer or speaker yourself. You have a creative imagination and may come across as an incurable romantic. You have strong intuition, maybe bordering on a mediumistic quality, which sets you apart from the mass. You may not be rich in cash terms, but your personal gifts are worth more than gold.

PISCES IN LOVE

Discover how compatible in love you are with people from the same and other signs of the zodiac. Five stars equals a match made in heaven!

Pisces meets Pisces

Pisceans are easy-going and get on well with most people, so when two Pisceans get together, harmony is invariably the result. While this isn't the most dynamic relationship, there is mutual understanding, and a desire to please on both sides. Neither partner is likely to be overbearing or selfish. Family responsibilities should be happily shared and home surroundings will be comfortable, but never pretentious. One of the better pairings for the sign of the Fishes. Star rating: *****

Pisces meets Aries

Still waters run deep, and they don't come much deeper than Pisces. Although these signs share the same quadrant of the zodiac, they have little in common. Pisces is a dreamer, a romantic idealist with steady and spiritual goals. Aries needs to be on the move, and has very different ideals. It's hard to see how a relationship could develop but, with patience, there is a chance that things might work out. Pisces needs incentive, and Aries may be the sign to offer it. Star rating: **

Pisces meets Taurus

No problem here, unless both parties come from the quieter side of their respective signs. Most of the time Taurus and Pisces would live comfortably together, offering mutual support and deep regard. Taurus can offer the personal qualities that Pisces craves, whilst Pisces understands and copes with the Bull's slightly stubborn qualities. Taurus is likely to travel in Piscean company, so there is a potential for wide-ranging experiences and variety which is essential. There will be some misunderstandings, mainly because Pisces is so deep, but that won't prevent their enduring happiness. Star rating: ***

Pisces meets Gemini

Gemini likes to think of itself as intuitive and intellectual, but it will never understand Pisces' dark depths. Another stumbling block is that both Gemini and Pisces are 'split' signs – the Twins and the two Fishes – which means that both are capable of dual personalities. There won't be any shortage of affection, but the real question has to be how much these people feel they have in common. Pisces is extremely kind, and so is Gemini most of the time. But Pisces does too much soul-searching for Gemini, who might eventually become bored. Star rating: ***

Pisces meets Cancer

This is likely to be a very successful match. Cancer and Pisces are both Water signs, both deep, sensitive and very caring. Pisces loves deeply, and Cancer wants to be loved. There will be few fireworks here, and a very quiet house. But that doesn't mean that either love or action is lacking – the latter of which is just behind closed doors. Family and children are important to both signs and both are prepared to work hard, but Pisces is the more restless of the two and needs the support and security that Cancer offers. Star rating: *****

Pisces meets Leo

Pisces always needs to understand others, which makes Leo feel warm and loved, while Leo sees, to its delight, that Pisces needs to be protected and taken care of. Pisceans are often lacking in self-confidence which is something Leo has to spare, and happily it is often infectious. Pisces' inevitable cares are swept away on a tide of Leonine cheerfulness. This couple's home would be cheerful and full of love, which is beneficial to all family members. This is not a meeting of minds, but rather an understanding and appreciation of differences. Star rating: ****

Pisces meets Virgo

This looks an unpromising match from beginning to end. There are exceptions to every rule, particularly where Pisces is concerned, but these two signs are both so deep it's hard to imagine that they could ever find what makes the other tick. The depth is different in each case: Virgo's ruminations are extremely materialistic, while Pisces exists in a world of deep-felt, poorly expressed emotion. Pisces and Virgo might find they don't talk much, so only in a contemplative, almost monastic, match would they ever get on. Still, in a vast zodiac, anything is possible. Star rating: **

Pisces meets Libra

Libra and Pisces can be extremely fond of each other, even deeply in love, but this alone isn't a stable foundation for long-term success. Pisces is extremely deep and doesn't even know itself very well. Libra may initially find this intriguing but will eventually feel frustrated at being unable to understand the Piscean's emotional and personal feelings. Pisces can be jealous and may find Libra's flightiness difficult, which Libra can't stand. They are great friends and they may make it to the romantic stakes, but when they get there a great deal of effort will be necessary. Star rating: ***

Pisces meets Scorpio

If ever there were two zodiac signs that have a total rapport, it has to be Scorpio and Pisces. They share very similar needs: they are not gregarious and are happy with a little silence, good music and time to contemplate the finer things in life, and both are attracted to family life. Apart, they can have a tendency to wander in a romantic sense, but this is reduced when they come together. They are deep, firm friends who enjoy each other's company and this must lead to an excellent chance of success. These people are surely made for each other! Star rating: *****

Pisces meets Sagittarius

Probably the least likely success story for either sign, which is why it scores so low on the star rating. The basic problem is an almost total lack of understanding. A successful relationship needs empathy and progress towards a shared goal but, although both are eager to please, Pisces is too deep and Sagittarius too flighty – they just don't belong on the same planet! As pals, they have more in common and so a friendship is the best hope of success and happiness. Star rating: *

Pisces meets Capricorn

There is some chance of a happy relationship here, but it will need work on both sides. Capricorn is a go-getter, but likes to plan long term. Pisces is naturally more immediate, but has enough intuition to understand the Goat's thinking. Both have patience, but it will usually be Pisces who chooses to play second fiddle. The quiet nature of both signs might be a problem, as someone will have to take the lead, especially in social situations. Both signs should recognise this fact and accommodate it. Star rating: ***

Pisces meets Aquarius

Zodiac signs that follow each other often have something in common, but this is often not the case with Aquarius and Pisces. Both signs are deeply caring, but in different ways. Pisces is one of the deepest zodiac signs, and Aquarius simply isn't prepared to embark on the journey. Pisceans, meanwhile, would probably find Aquarians superficial and even flippant. On the positive side, there is potential for a well-balanced relationship, but unless one party is untypical of their zodiac sign, it often doesn't get started. Star rating: **

VENUS:
THE PLANET OF LOVE

If you look up at the sky around sunset or sunrise you will often see Venus in close attendance to the Sun. It is arguably one of the most beautiful sights of all and there is little wonder that historically it became associated with the goddess of love. But although Venus does play an important part in the way you view love and in the way others see you romantically, this is only one of the spheres of influence that it enjoys in your overall character.

Venus has a part to play in the more cultured side of your life and has much to do with your appreciation of art, literature, music and general creativity. Even the way you look is responsive to the part of the zodiac that Venus occupied at the start of your life, though this fact is also down to your Sun sign and Ascending sign. If, at the time you were born, Venus occupied one of the more gregarious zodiac signs, you will be more likely to wear your heart on your sleeve, as well as to be more attracted to entertainment, social gatherings and good company. If on the other hand Venus occupied a quiet zodiac sign at the time of your birth, you would tend to be more retiring and less willing to shine in public situations.

It's good to know what part the planet Venus plays in your life for it can have a great bearing on the way you appear to the rest of the world and since we all have to mix with others, you can learn to make the very best of what Venus has to offer you.

One of the great complications in the past has always been trying to establish exactly what zodiac position Venus enjoyed when you were born because the planet is notoriously difficult to track. However, we have solved that problem by creating a table that is exclusive to your Sun sign, which you will find on the following page.

Establishing your Venus sign could not be easier. Just look up the year of your birth on the following page and you will see a sign of the zodiac. This was the sign that Venus occupied in the period covered by your sign in that year. If Venus occupied more than one sign during the period, this is indicated by the date on which the sign changed, and the name of the new sign. For instance, if you were born in 1940, Venus was in Aries until the 9th March, after which time it was in Taurus. If you were born before 9th March your Venus sign is Aries, if you were born on or after 9th March, your Venus sign is Taurus. Once you have established the position of Venus at the time of your birth, you can then look in the pages which follow to see how this has a bearing on your life as a whole.

1912 CAPRICORN / 24.2 AQUARIUS / 19.3 PISCES
1913 ARIES / 7.3 TAURUS
1914 PISCES / 15.3 ARIES
1915 CAPRICORN
1916 ARIES / 10.3 TAURUS
1917 AQUARIUS / 5.3 PISCES
1918 AQUARIUS
1919 PISCES / 27.2 ARIES
1920 CAPRICORN / 24.2 AQUARIUS / 19.3 PISCES
1921 ARIES / 8.3 TAURUS
1922 PISCES / 14.3 ARIES
1923 CAPRICORN
1924 ARIES / 10.3 TAURUS
1925 AQUARIUS / 4.3 PISCES
1926 AQUARIUS
1927 PISCES / 26.2 ARIES
1928 CAPRICORN / 23.2 AQUARIUS / 18.3 PISCES
1929 ARIES / 9.3 TAURUS
1930 PISCES / 13.3 ARIES
1931 CAPRICORN
1932 ARIES / 9.3 TAURUS
1933 AQUARIUS / 4.3 PISCES
1934 AQUARIUS
1935 PISCES / 25.2 ARIES
1936 CAPRICORN / 23.2 AQUARIUS / 18.3 PISCES
1937 ARIES / 10.3 TAURUS
1938 PISCES / 12.3 ARIES
1939 CAPRICORN
1940 ARIES / 9.3 TAURUS
1941 AQUARIUS / 3.3 PISCES
1942 AQUARIUS
1943 PISCES / 25.2 ARIES
1944 CAPRICORN / 22.2 AQUARIUS / 18.3 PISCES
1945 ARIES / 11.3 TAURUS
1946 PISCES / 11.3 ARIES
1947 CAPRICORN
1948 ARIES / 8.3 TAURUS
1949 AQUARIUS / 3.3 PISCES
1950 AQUARIUS
1951 PISCES / 24.2 ARIES
1952 CAPRICORN / 22.2 AQUARIUS / 17.3 PISCES
1953 ARIES
1954 PISCES / 11.3 ARIES
1955 CAPRICORN
1956 ARIES / 8.3 TAURUS
1957 AQUARIUS / 2.3 PISCES
1958 CAPRICORN / 25.2 AQUARIUS
1959 PISCES / 24.2 ARIES
1960 CAPRICORN / 21.2 AQUARIUS / 17.3 PISCES
1961 ARIES
1962 PISCES / 10.3 ARIES
1963 CAPRICORN
1964 ARIES / 8.3 TAURUS
1965 AQUARIUS / 1.3 PISCES
1966 AQUARIUS
1967 PISCES / 23.2 ARIES
1968 SAGITTARIUS / 26.1 CAPRICORN
1969 ARIES
1970 PISCES / 10.3 ARIES
1971 CAPRICORN
1972 ARIES / 7.3 TAURUS
1973 AQUARIUS / 1.3 PISCES
1974 CAPRICORN / 2.3 AQUARIUS
1975 PISCES / 23.2 ARIES
1976 SAGITTARIUS / 26.1 CAPRICORN
1977 ARIES
1978 PISCES / 9.3 ARIES
1979 CAPRICORN
1980 ARIES / 7.3 TAURUS
1981 AQUARIUS / 28.2 PISCES
1982 CAPRICORN / 4.3 AQUARIUS
1983 PISCES / 23.2 ARIES
1984 SAGITTARIUS / 25.1 CAPRICORN
1985 ARIES
1986 PISCES / 9.3 ARIES
1987 CAPRICORN
1988 ARIES / 7.3 TAURUS
1989 AQUARIUS / 28.2 PISCES
1990 CAPRICORN / 5.3 AQUARIUS
1991 PISCES / 22.2 ARIES / 20.3 TAURUS
1992 SAGITTARIUS / 25.1 CAPRICORN
1993 ARIES
1994 PISCES / 9.3 ARIES
1995 CAPRICORN
1996 ARIES / 7.3 TAURUS
1997 AQUARIUS / 27.2 PISCES
1998 CAPRICORN / 5.3 AQUARIUS
1999 PISCES / 22.2 ARIES / 19.3 TAURUS
2000 SAGITTARIUS / 25.1 CAPRICORN
2001 ARIES
2002 PISCES / 9.3 ARIES
2003 CAPRICORN
2004 ARIES / 7.3 TAURUS
2005 AQUARIUS / 27.2 PISCES
2006 CAPRICORN / 5.3 AQUARIUS
2007 PISCES / 22.2 ARIES
2008 SAGITTARIUS / 25.1 CAPRICORN
2009 ARIES
2010 PISCES / 9.3 ARIES

VENUS THROUGH THE ZODIAC SIGNS

Venus in Aries

Amongst other things, the position of Venus in Aries indicates a fondness for travel, music and all creative pursuits. Your nature tends to be affectionate and you would try not to create confusion or difficulty for others if it could be avoided. Many people with this planetary position have a great love of the theatre, and mental stimulation is of the greatest importance. Early romantic attachments are common with Venus in Aries, so it is very important to establish a genuine sense of romantic continuity. Early marriage is not recommended, especially if it is based on sympathy. You may give your heart a little too readily on occasions.

Venus in Taurus

You are capable of very deep feelings and your emotions tend to last for a very long time. This makes you a trusting partner and lover, whose constancy is second to none. In life you are precise and careful and always try to do things the right way. Although this means an ordered life, which you are comfortable with, it can also lead you to be rather too fussy for your own good. Despite your pleasant nature, you are very fixed in your opinions and quite able to speak your mind. Others are attracted to you and historical astrologers always quoted this position of Venus as being very fortunate in terms of marriage. However, if you find yourself involved in a failed relationship, it could take you a long time to trust again.

Venus in Gemini

As with all associations related to Gemini, you tend to be quite versatile, anxious for change and intelligent in your dealings with the world at large. You may gain money from more than one source but you are equally good at spending it. There is an inference here that you are a good communicator, via either the written or the spoken word, and you love to be in the company of interesting people. Always on the look-out for culture, you may also be very fond of music, and love to indulge the curious and cultured side of your nature. In romance you tend to have more than one relationship and could find yourself associated with someone who has previously been a friend or even a distant relative.

Venus in Cancer

You often stay close to home because you are very fond of family and enjoy many of your most treasured moments when you are with those you love. Being naturally sympathetic, you will always do anything you can to support those around you, even people you hardly know at all. This charitable side of your nature is your most noticeable trait and is one of the reasons why others are naturally so fond of you. Being receptive and in some cases even psychic, you can see through to the soul of most of those with whom you come into contact. You may not commence too many romantic attachments but when you do give your heart, it tends to be unconditionally.

Venus in Leo

It must become quickly obvious to almost anyone you meet that you are kind, sympathetic and yet determined enough to stand up for anyone or anything that is truly important to you. Bright and sunny, you warm the world with your natural enthusiasm and would rarely do anything to hurt those around you, or at least not intentionally. In romance you are ardent and sincere, though some may find your style just a little overpowering. Gains come through your contacts with other people and this could be especially true with regard to romance, for love and money often come hand in hand for those who were born with Venus in Leo. People claim to understand you, though you are more complex than you seem.

Venus in Virgo

Your nature could well be fairly quiet no matter what your Sun sign might be, though this fact often manifests itself as an inner peace and would not prevent you from being basically sociable. Some delays and even the odd disappointment in love cannot be ruled out with this planetary position, though it's a fact that you will usually find the happiness you look for in the end. Catapulting yourself into romantic entanglements that you know to be rather ill-advised is not sensible, and it would be better to wait before you committed yourself exclusively to any one person. It is the essence of your nature to serve the world at large and through doing so it is possible that you will attract money at some stage in your life.

Venus in Libra

Venus is very comfortable in Libra and bestows upon those people who have this planetary position a particular sort of kindness that is easy to recognise. This is a very good position for all sorts of friendships and also for romantic attachments that usually bring much joy into your life. Few individuals with Venus in Libra would avoid marriage and since you are capable of great depths of love, it is likely that you will find a contented personal life. You like to mix with people of integrity and intelligence but don't take kindly to scruffy surroundings or work that means getting your hands too dirty. Careful speculation, good business dealings and money through marriage all seem fairly likely.

Venus in Scorpio

You are quite open and tend to spend money quite freely, even on those occasions when you don't have very much. Although your intentions are always good, there are times when you get yourself in to the odd scrape and this can be particularly true when it comes to romance, which you may come to late or from a rather unexpected direction. Certainly you have the power to be happy and to make others contented on the way, but you find the odd stumbling block on your journey through life and it could seem that you have to work harder than those around you. As a result of this, you gain a much deeper understanding of the true value of personal happiness than many people ever do, and are likely to achieve true contentment in the end.

Venus in Sagittarius

You are lighthearted, cheerful and always able to see the funny side of any situation. These facts enhance your popularity, which is especially high with members of the opposite sex. You should never have to look too far to find romantic interest in your life, though it is just possible that you might be too willing to commit yourself before you are certain that the person in question is right for you. Part of the problem here extends to other areas of life too. The fact is that you like variety in everything and so can tire of situations that fail to offer it. All the same, if you choose wisely and learn to understand your restless side, then great happiness can be yours.

Venus in Capricorn

The most notable trait that comes from Venus in this position is that it makes you trustworthy and able to take on all sorts of responsibilities in life. People are instinctively fond of you and love you all the more because you are always ready to help those who are in any form of need. Social and business popularity can be yours and there is a magnetic quality to your nature that is particularly attractive in a romantic sense. Anyone who wants a partner for a lover, a spouse and a good friend too would almost certainly look in your direction. Constancy is the hallmark of your nature and unfaithfulness would go right against the grain. You might sometimes be a little too trusting.

Venus in Aquarius

This location of Venus offers a fondness for travel and a desire to try out something new at every possible opportunity. You are extremely easy to get along with and tend to have many friends from varied backgrounds, classes and inclinations. You like to live a distinct sort of life and gain a great deal from moving about, both in a career sense and with regard to your home. It is not out of the question that you could form a romantic attachment to someone who comes from far away or be attracted to a person of a distinctly artistic and original nature. What you cannot stand is jealousy, for you have friends of both sexes and would want to keep things that way.

Venus in Pisces

The first thing people tend to notice about you is your wonderful, warm smile. Being very charitable by nature you will do anything to help others, even if you don't know them well. Much of your life may be spent sorting out situations for other people, but it is very important to feel that you are living for yourself too. In the main, you remain cheerful, and tend to be quite attractive to members of the opposite sex. Where romantic attachments are concerned, you could be drawn to people who are significantly older or younger than yourself or to someone with a unique career or point of view. It might be best for you to avoid marrying whilst you are still very young.

PISCES:
2009 DIARY PAGES

October 2009

1 THURSDAY
Moon Age Day 12 Moon Sign Pisces

Look for a definite window of opportunity as the lunar high arrives today and use it in order to get ahead of the crowd. Almost anyone you meet might turn out to be pivotal to your plans and therefore your future, so you have to keep paying attention. This could well be a very busy day, but one that could offer you far more than you have been expecting.

2 FRIDAY
Moon Age Day 13 Moon Sign Pisces

The promising period continues, and today is one of those days during which you create your own good luck as you go along. New dreams and schemes are there for the taking, and these can help you to move closer to your heart's desire. In romantic situations you have all the golden words necessary to knock someone right off their feet.

3 SATURDAY
Moon Age Day 14 Moon Sign Pisces

Do be ready to get rid of any dead wood that has been accumulating in your life recently. The path ahead of you seems quite clear, and you shouldn't be lacking when it comes to using initiative and even cunning. An ideal time to welcome people you don't see very often back into your life across the weekend, and to enjoy what they can bring.

4 SUNDAY
Moon Age Day 15 Moon Sign Aries

Trends support a great urge on your part to get on well with others and to involve them more and more in your plans. Today is all about seeing well ahead of yourself in most situations and backing your intuition. Some people might even call you psychic at the moment, because it is so easy for you to assess how any particular situation will turn out.

5 MONDAY *Moon Age Day 16   Moon Sign Aries*

You are a zodiac sign with a natural talent for communication at the moment. Mercury is in a really good position in your chart and it should help you to keep chatting on throughout the whole day and beyond. You might even talk in your sleep, so keen are you at the moment to let people know how you really feel about everything.

6 TUESDAY *Moon Age Day 17   Moon Sign Taurus*

The scope for personal freedom is strong and there are good rewards to be had from letting the world know that you are available and ready to take action. There may be occasions when you need to be rather forceful in the way you get your message across, and that could shock those who are used to your quiet ways.

7 WEDNESDAY *Moon Age Day 18   Moon Sign Taurus*

Keeping relationships harmonious is the name of the game, and you can afford to let romance colour your attitudes and your day right now. At this stage of the week your best approach is to watch and wait, and to remain willing to co-operate at work and to compromise if it proves to be necessary. Reap the benefits of allowing new personalities into your life.

8 THURSDAY *Moon Age Day 19   Moon Sign Gemini*

Change for the better is something you can now accomplish quite easily if you keep your mind clear and your attitudes sound and reasonable. Even if not everyone you deal with is quite as fair and open-minded as you are, the focus is on your ability to show just how patient you can be, which could prove to be very important.

9 FRIDAY *Moon Age Day 20   Moon Sign Gemini*

It's worth trying to glean important information from your partner or those to whom you are particularly close. Be prepared to keep your eyes and ears open because it is possible to help yourself at every stage of today. Make the most of opportunities to use your skills to clarify and resolve issues, particularly if others seem rather confused!

YOUR DAILY GUIDE TO OCTOBER 2009

10 SATURDAY   *Moon Age Day 21   Moon Sign Gemini*

Powerful ego tendencies now begin to show, and although these could cause you the odd problem, in the main they offer you scope to show how much you are enjoying life and how capable you actually are when it comes to getting things done. Even if not everyone wants to be your friend today, you can persuade those people you care about to adore you.

11 SUNDAY   *Moon Age Day 22   Moon Sign Cancer*

This would be an ideal period to sort out certain aspects of your life and to make sure that what is going on around you is what you really need. This may not be universally the case and some adjustments could be necessary. Even if you turn this into a practical sort of Sunday, there ought to be room for enjoyment too, perhaps with your family.

12 MONDAY   *Moon Age Day 23   Moon Sign Cancer*

The spotlight is on bringing matters at work to a satisfactory conclusion and on solving any problems that have been dogging you for a while. There are many insights available to you around now, and a good deal of coming and going may well be necessary in order to get all those important details right.

13 TUESDAY   *Moon Age Day 24   Moon Sign Leo*

You may now desire to change your personal lifestyle, but do you have everything in place to make this possible? It is important to look at the details and to make sure everything is organised in the way you want it to be. Joint business matters are to the fore, and the thought of financial gain can be very inspiring!

14 WEDNESDAY   *Moon Age Day 25   Moon Sign Leo*

You would be wise to keep up your efforts for today and make sure that all necessary jobs are done before tomorrow. The lunar low is on its way and this time around it can offer a complete break and a retreat from some of life's pressures. This is necessary on occasions so that you can recharge your batteries and get the rest your body requires.

YOUR DAILY GUIDE TO OCTOBER 2009

15 THURSDAY *Moon Age Day 26   Moon Sign Virgo*

You may decide there is no sense in trying too hard today because you would simply be knocking your head against a brick wall. You can afford to let others take the strain while you sit back and enjoy the show. Staying close to home when it is possible to do so would be no bad thing, and any new projects are probably best left until the weekend.

16 FRIDAY *Moon Age Day 27   Moon Sign Virgo*

For once your people skills may not be highlighted. This isn't like you at all, but your accustomed intuition is now less evident than usual, as is your patience. Even if this isn't the best end to the working week you have ever experienced, you should at least have kept your powder dry for later efforts. By the evening you can make sure things are looking better.

17 SATURDAY *Moon Age Day 28   Moon Sign Libra*

There is much to be said for breaking with some of your usual routines and trying out newer and more interesting possibilities. Just make sure that you don't throw out the baby with the bathwater. It might seem at first as if a certain ruthlessness is required, but if this really isn't your style, it may not work very well.

18 SUNDAY *Moon Age Day 0   Moon Sign Libra*

Once more you have scope to transform your personal life. This doesn't necessarily mean dumping relationships or insisting on changing everything for the sake of it. What is much more likely is that you are setting new trains in motion and then watching closely to see what happens. This evening brings strong social inclinations.

19 MONDAY *Moon Age Day 1   Moon Sign Scorpio*

You can now easily influence other people with your views and with the way you are talking. An inspirational approach works best, and should be appreciated by others. You need to be aware of any coincidences that crop up today. Some of these can act as signposts to show you whether your life is going in exactly the right direction.

20 TUESDAY *Moon Age Day 2   Moon Sign Scorpio*

Your need to analyse and to probe is highlighted more than ever, and that famous Piscean curiosity is assisting you to put yourself in potentially fortunate situations. Answering questions can now be your forte, and you can put this skill to good use if colleagues and friends turn to you for advice. What matters the most now is your originality.

21 WEDNESDAY *Moon Age Day 3   Moon Sign Sagittarius*

Now is the time to dispense with some of the usual formalities and cut right to the chase. This can help you to achieve a generally successful day and assist you to make gains you may not have even expected. Money matters can be made more settled, and you have chances to make gains from relatively unexpected directions.

22 THURSDAY *Moon Age Day 4   Moon Sign Sagittarius*

You generally have a good psychological understanding of your own nature and those of the people with whom you interact. This is especially true at the moment, and it allows you to second-guess the way they are likely to react under any given circumstance. Your ability to solve problems can make all the difference now.

23 FRIDAY *Moon Age Day 5   Moon Sign Sagittarius*

Create some opportunities today to understand those around you and to enjoy special times with your lover. For those Pisces subjects who are presently between relationships, there is much you can do to change the situation. A new love is definitely possible, but you need to ask yourself whether you are happier on your own at the moment.

24 SATURDAY *Moon Age Day 6   Moon Sign Capricorn*

You have what it takes to be both adventurous and optimistic across the weekend and to move the odd mountain if the desire to do so takes your fancy. There is also an emphasis on your level of physical motivation. Whatever you decide to take on today will work out best if you maintain your great determination.

25 SUNDAY
Moon Age Day 7   Moon Sign Capricorn

Even if you feel slightly more impatient today, you needn't let that take the edge off your competitive instincts at all – in fact it could heighten them. By all means do whatever you can to obtain your objectives, though you could lose friends on the way if you are too ruthless. Such phases as this never last long for peaceful Pisces.

26 MONDAY
Moon Age Day 8   Moon Sign Aquarius

You should be able to ensure that relationships are working out especially well at the beginning of this week. At the same time you are entering a slightly dreamy phase for the next couple of days, and it may be difficult to keep yourself motivated or physically inclined. Learn that a great deal can also be gained from meditating and waiting in the wings.

27 TUESDAY
Moon Age Day 9   Moon Sign Aquarius

This is a time to allow wider interests to enter your life, even if you are looking at the possibilities in a slightly low-key way for the moment. There should be time to make up your mind and less pressure being placed upon you than was the case earlier in the month. All in all you can afford to feel quite good about yourself around now.

28 WEDNESDAY
Moon Age Day 10   Moon Sign Aquarius

Today is about being gentle on yourself and also kind in the way you approach the world at large. Make sure this fact is not lost on other people. Although there will always be some folk around who take advantage of your good nature, in the main this will not be the case. Get onside with colleagues who have ambitious plans and show your support.

29 THURSDAY
Moon Age Day 11   Moon Sign Pisces

The lunar high assists you to make the most of any career opportunities that are available. It is important to pay attention because many benefits today will come like a bolt from the blue. This is the time of the month when you have to realise that life is not a rehearsal and that what you get out of it is directly responsive to what you have first put in.

YOUR DAILY GUIDE TO OCTOBER 2009

30 FRIDAY *Moon Age Day 12   Moon Sign Pisces*

You can rely on your personal charm to a great extent today and you should discover that Lady Luck has more than a small part to play in your fortunes. This is particularly the case if you can grab opportunities as they come along and remain wide-awake to all of them. A day to tap into the friendship and support of those around you.

31 SATURDAY *Moon Age Day 13   Moon Sign Aries*

This is the ideal time to reflect for a little while on what has happened during October and how you can best use any good fortune that has come your way in order to get on better later. There should also be time for a good heart-to-heart with your partner or a family member who needs your support. By all means give advice, but avoid taking over.

November 2009

1 SUNDAY
Moon Age Day 14   Moon Sign Aries

When it comes to the practical side of your nature the focus is on your good ideas and your knowledge of how to put them into practice. Rather than worrying about inconsequential details today, why not simply get on with doing what you know is correct? Even if others express doubts, you have what it takes to smile and carry on anyway.

2 MONDAY
Moon Age Day 15   Moon Sign Aries

Working on business projects could be interesting, though there are times today when you may decide you are happy to let others take the strain whilst you find newer and better ways to get things done. The fact is that you can be inspirational at present, and should be ready to show an unsuspecting world that you can achieve much when left to get on with it.

3 TUESDAY
Moon Age Day 16   Moon Sign Taurus

In terms of your mental skills you should be sharp as a pin, and it would probably take someone extremely clever to pull the wool over your eyes at present. New ideas and breakthroughs are definitely possible, and you seem to be entering a phase that allows you to take control to a much greater extent. If you need support today, why not ask friends?

4 WEDNESDAY
Moon Age Day 17   Moon Sign Taurus

Trends indicate that any plan of action might need addressing and maybe altering, even before you have really got started. Actually that is the time to make changes because once things really get going you will be too occupied. Pisces is rarely as go-getting as it is at present, so rather than standing around waiting, it's time to get stuck in!

5 THURSDAY
Moon Age Day 18   Moon Sign Gemini

You should now be in a position to gain help in the form of very special relationships you enjoy with specific individuals, either at work or in a social sense. It's natural to turn to those who have been friends for a very long time and therefore people you know you can trust. However, even strangers have their part to play today or tomorrow.

6 FRIDAY
Moon Age Day 19   Moon Sign Gemini

There is a strong emphasis on both social and romantic possibilities as the working week draws to its close. If you are looking for love, don't be afraid to consider methods you haven't tried before in order to get to meet the right person. The extreme warmth and kindness of all Pisces people should be apparent under present trends.

7 SATURDAY
Moon Age Day 20   Moon Sign Cancer

Intellectual and philosophical interests are the order of the day for at least some of your time as the weekend gets started. At the same time you may well have itchy feet, and a shopping spree with friends would be no bad thing. Christmas isn't very far away, so the time is right to look for some real bargains. Spending wisely is the key at present.

8 SUNDAY
Moon Age Day 21   Moon Sign Cancer

It might be all too easy today to get at cross-purposes with people you need to charm, particularly if you haven't checked on certain details or facts. The way you approach others is now extremely important because there are people around who can offer you so much. Today is much more about physicality than spirituality.

9 MONDAY
Moon Age Day 22   Moon Sign Leo

In a social sense there may be a few ups and downs to deal with right now. There is much to be said for getting out there and doing new things. If circumstances hold you back or dictate that you are stuck in one place all the time, a little frustration could follow. This is a week to take charge of your own destiny if at all possible.

YOUR DAILY GUIDE TO NOVEMBER 2009

10 TUESDAY *Moon Age Day 23 Moon Sign Leo*

Now you need to find constructive outlets for the masses of energy that you have at your disposal. Whilst other zodiac signs find difficulty with the onset of the winter, you should be able to cope with it very well indeed. At work this would be an ideal time to take a step up the ladder of advancement, even if you have doubts about this.

11 WEDNESDAY *Moon Age Day 24 Moon Sign Virgo*

Don't be too surprised if circumstances seem to hold you back today. The lunar low comes along, giving you no assistance in your efforts to do what comes naturally. This is not to suggest that your own choices are impossible, but extra effort will be required. Make full use of your inquisitive mind and your desire to find out specific facts.

12 THURSDAY *Moon Age Day 25 Moon Sign Virgo*

Situations of one sort or another could well try your patience now, and you may not have the level of tolerance for which your zodiac sign is justifiably famous. On the plus side, there are good reasons to agitate for things you consider are absolutely vital, and you needn't take no for an answer when you are certain of your ground.

13 FRIDAY *Moon Age Day 26 Moon Sign Libra*

Capitalise on a more light-hearted trend that starts now the lunar low is out of the way. It might be increasingly hard for you to take anything very seriously and you need to take full advantage of the many new ideas that are available around now. Opportunities for long-distance travel are particularly well starred at the moment.

14 SATURDAY *Moon Age Day 27 Moon Sign Libra*

The way you approach your life in a general sense enables you to bring happiness to others, sometimes at the expense of your own desires. This is less likely to be true at present because you clearly have what it takes to make everyone else comfortable with their lives, whilst at the same time finding contentment yourself.

YOUR DAILY GUIDE TO NOVEMBER 2009

15 SUNDAY *Moon Age Day 28   Moon Sign Scorpio*

You need to find new input in order to make sure that some of your most cherished plans are not going to falter. It is important for you to feel that things generally are working out as you have intended, even if an extra push is necessary here and there. Why not use at least part of today to spend time proving your affection romantically?

16 MONDAY *Moon Age Day 29   Moon Sign Scorpio*

By all means focus your energies on professional matters but learn to leave these alone once the working day is over. There is much more to your life than practical considerations and especially so under present planetary trends. New friendships are possible, together with an important realisation regarding someone you already know.

17 TUESDAY *Moon Age Day 0   Moon Sign Scorpio*

The focus is on travel whilst the Sun remains in your solar ninth house, perhaps to exotic or distant places. Trends also enhance your intellectual curiosity, encouraging you to persevere in order to get to the bottom of puzzles or issues. Even people can stimulate your mind, and it is suddenly very important to know their motivations.

18 WEDNESDAY *Moon Age Day 1   Moon Sign Sagittarius*

You can turn this into another favourable time as far as your career is concerned. If you know exactly how things ought to be going, you should be doing all you can to alter circumstances to suit your mental pattern. It shouldn't be hard to get others involved in your schemes, and it seems as if everyone wants to be on your team now.

19 THURSDAY *Moon Age Day 2   Moon Sign Sagittarius*

You can get the best from most situations simply by being what nature made you. Today is about putting your natural kindness on display, and you have what it takes to inspire colleagues and friends. Make the most of the popularity you are able to achieve, and the fact that your smiling face is dear to all sorts of individuals, some of whom you don't even count as being particular friends.

YOUR DAILY GUIDE TO NOVEMBER 2009

20 FRIDAY *Moon Age Day 3   Moon Sign Capricorn*

The Moon has now moved into your solar eleventh house, and for a day or two you might seem slightly more distant and difficult for others to understand. There's nothing wrong with retreating more into your own world, though it might be a journey that others simply cannot take. You should still be aware of how to complete practical demands.

21 SATURDAY *Moon Age Day 4   Moon Sign Capricorn*

You needn't let anything get in the way of your intellectual curiosity at this time, even if you express it in a slightly quieter way than you did a few days ago. If you really do need to know why situations are the way they are, this is an ideal time to turn over stones on the path of life, simply so you can find out what might be hiding beneath them.

22 SUNDAY *Moon Age Day 5   Moon Sign Capricorn*

The Moon in your solar twelfth house now offers a somewhat quieter interlude than usual, and friends might wonder if there is something bothering you. Even if this is not the case, you may well decide you don't have the same need for company as you usually do. One option is simply to remain alone today.

23 MONDAY *Moon Age Day 6   Moon Sign Aquarius*

You can afford to make work the single most important motivating factor for the moment, and to let your social life take a back seat until the middle of the week. Today works best if you only deal with one major situation at a time and are willing leave everything else alone. An inability to multi-task is the most evident result.

24 TUESDAY *Moon Age Day 7   Moon Sign Aquarius*

Meetings with others can help you expand your horizons no end, and you can slowly but surely come out of your shell as the Moon moves towards your zodiac sign of Pisces. Hour by hour you will be demonstrating your ability to think logically but also to bear in mind that tremendous Piscean intuition. Allow people to marvel at your insights.

25 WEDNESDAY *Moon Age Day 8 Moon Sign Pisces*

The lunar high can be especially fruitful this month and assists you to move closer than ever to getting something important working in your life. At the same time you have what it takes to inspire others to work on your behalf, which they should do quite naturally because of their affection for you. Finances can also be strengthened now.

26 THURSDAY *Moon Age Day 9 Moon Sign Pisces*

Prepare to pursue success and to get things going your way. This shouldn't simply be a case of better luck, because you have what it takes to put in so much extra effort that you deserve to succeed. You can even persuade those who have not been on your side in the recent past to understand your true motivations and to join forces with you.

27 FRIDAY *Moon Age Day 10 Moon Sign Pisces*

Trends assist you to make all the right moves, especially at work. If you are presently involved in full-time education you should be able to find out something to your advantage, and all Pisceans can take advantage of better financial prospects quite soon. Look out for a magnetic stranger who might have something to offer you.

28 SATURDAY *Moon Age Day 11 Moon Sign Aries*

By all means enjoy the successes you have achieved in different spheres of your life, though it has to be said that you may also be filled with burning desires that are not too easy to address or to achieve. It is so often the case that at the core of Pisces there is a divine discontent, often brought about because of slightly unrealistic expectations.

29 SUNDAY *Moon Age Day 12 Moon Sign Aries*

Freedom can be the key to happiness at present and there isn't much doubt that you will be at your best when you have hours in front of you to spend doing whatever takes your fancy. Not that you need to spend these alone. Your social motivation is strong, and you can use it to get yourself involved in joyful events.

30 MONDAY — Moon Age Day 13 — Moon Sign Taurus

The focus is on your increased self-confidence and a desire to have things work out the way you expect. All the more reason to refuse to take no for an answer when it comes to social invitations you are handing out. Many Piscean individuals will already be laying down quite detailed plans for the holiday period.

December 2009

1 TUESDAY
Moon Age Day 14   Moon Sign Taurus

Just discovering new possibilities could be pleasurable enough but right now you have scope to take things one stage further. You have what it takes to build on what you discover and to make others happier as a result. This might be a rather outlandish ambition, but it is part of what makes you who you are. Be prepared to seek support from friends.

2 WEDNESDAY
Moon Age Day 15   Moon Sign Gemini

Today you can make use of extra vigour and work harder as a result. Make sure that what you are doing is going to benefit you later on because there isn't sufficient time to be going down blind alleys at the moment. The time is right to offer words of love to your partner, and practical help to anyone who has need of your very special skills.

3 THURSDAY
Moon Age Day 16   Moon Sign Gemini

A much quieter and less demanding interlude is available as the Moon enters your solar fourth house. This also assists you to project yourself directly into the warmth of your family circle, where you can achieve real contentment. There is a little trepidation in the mind of some Pisceans, maybe regarding a possible confrontation later.

4 FRIDAY
Moon Age Day 17   Moon Sign Cancer

In an emotional sense you might remain locked inside yourself, though you needn't allow this to show practically if you insist to the world at large that you are capable and very willing to get involved. Splitting your nature in this way is not at all unusual for Pisces, and you are able to fool anyone with your apparent confidence and dynamism.

YOUR DAILY GUIDE TO DECEMBER 2009

5 SATURDAY *Moon Age Day 18   Moon Sign Cancer*

There is much to be said for seeking a little romance now and the signs are very good when it comes to affairs of the heart. You can make this a secure and happy sort of weekend, particularly if other people are doing all they can to please you. Don't hold back when it comes to speaking those important words that mean so much to others.

6 SUNDAY *Moon Age Day 19   Moon Sign Leo*

If you have anything to teach others at the moment – and chances are you do – this is best achieved by example. Even when you lack some confidence in your own abilities you needn't demonstrate the fact, and should appear to be absolutely certain of everything. It's worth finishing today on a social footing by getting together with good friends.

7 MONDAY *Moon Age Day 20   Moon Sign Leo*

It could help today to pay attention to the finer details of life, especially where work is concerned. Don't worry if others aren't too keen on the way you present yourself – if you know it works, do it! You can't be flavour of the month with everyone at the moment, but should make the most of the fact that at least some people appreciate you.

8 TUESDAY *Moon Age Day 21   Moon Sign Virgo*

It's time to streamline your life and to focus only on what really matters. With the lunar low around you cannot afford to tackle too many jobs at the same time, even if there is an urge within you to feel as though something is being achieved. A little pretence may be necessary on those occasions when true confidence is lacking.

9 WEDNESDAY *Moon Age Day 22   Moon Sign Virgo*

The lunar low could encourage you to give way to some sloppy thinking, so it is worthwhile testing your ideas before you put them into practice. Don't be afraid to seek assistance if you need it, even if it means having to trawl around more than you really want to at the moment. Not the best day of the month – but keep trying!

10 THURSDAY *Moon Age Day 23   Moon Sign Libra*

You should now be in a better position for organising yourself at a practical level. Professional headway is easier to achieve and there are new and better incentives waiting in the wings. This could certainly be a favourable day as far as romance is concerned, particularly if you are willing to show your affection to a much greater extent.

11 FRIDAY *Moon Age Day 24   Moon Sign Libra*

There is only so much you can control today, so if you know in your heart that you are trying to do too much, now is the time to slow things down. It would be far better to do a couple of jobs well today than to do a dozen things badly. Anything you can't address today can wait until later in the month and could be better for the delay.

12 SATURDAY *Moon Age Day 25   Moon Sign Libra*

Socially speaking trends indicate a definite thirst for freedom and excitement. Perhaps Pisces is developing the Christmas spirit already, and this would not be particularly surprising because this is a time of year you relish. Your best approach is to join in the fun wherever you find it and arrange some sort of get-together yourself if possible.

13 SUNDAY *Moon Age Day 26   Moon Sign Scorpio*

There ought to be plenty of opportunity to expand your social horizons and today offers newer and better opportunities for you to make a really good impression all round. This is also an ideal time to plan your strategy for the coming week, and to make certain everything is in place in terms of your career.

14 MONDAY *Moon Age Day 27   Moon Sign Scorpio*

You can get your own way today primarily through the use of your charm, which is always the greatest weapon in the Piscean armoury. You can put your talents to especially good use in a career setting and should be on form when it comes to exploiting newer and better ideas. At home you can now ensure that romance begins to blossom.

15 TUESDAY *Moon Age Day 28   Moon Sign Sagittarius*

In a professional sense you are now entering a more dynamic phase all round, which might be something of a pity with Christmas just around the corner. All the same you can make significant progress and should be anxious to exploit your talents to the full. Routines could be a bit of bind, especially if they prevent you from motoring on.

16 WEDNESDAY *Moon Age Day 0   Moon Sign Sagittarius*

Things could well be on a hair trigger when it comes to relationships, and it's worth being especially careful not to offer unintended offence to people who are too sensitive for their own good. This is less inclined to happen at home, particularly if relationships there are settled and happy. Be ready to address the needs of friends.

17 THURSDAY *Moon Age Day 1   Moon Sign Capricorn*

You will have a sense of being virtually driven by your need to exploit new opportunities in your life and because of this you might not be giving as much attention as usual to the impending festivities. Social events could change your attitude, particularly if you are willing to be the life and soul of just about any party around now.

18 FRIDAY *Moon Age Day 2   Moon Sign Capricorn*

You can keep things moving forward under present astrological trends and there is no sign of life slowing down at any time now. On the contrary, you may be burning the candle at both ends and that could mean fatigue unless you are careful. Who knows where new possibilities will lead? Life should be very exciting.

19 SATURDAY *Moon Age Day 3   Moon Sign Capricorn*

Even if you continue to show your best and most organised face to the world, you could stumble when you come across anyone who doesn't respond to your charm. There are always going to be those who are immune to your delightful personality but in the rush to achieve even greater success you may simply have to ignore them.

20 SUNDAY   *Moon Age Day 4*   *Moon Sign Aquarius*

Mars is now in your solar sixth house, assisting you to show greater and greater effectiveness when it matters the most. If anything, you might be slightly hampered by the fact that you can't do anything too practical on a Sunday. At the same time, getting into Christmas mode with others can make all the difference.

21 MONDAY   *Moon Age Day 5*   *Moon Sign Aquarius*

Getting your own way remains generally simple and is down to a combination of determination and your naturally winning ways. It's all about knowing that what you believe is right, and when you have true conviction on your side you are unlikely to be stopped. Social moments could be quieter, but a romantic interlude is still possible.

22 TUESDAY   *Moon Age Day 6*   *Moon Sign Pisces*

Continuing to succeed and to move forward is simply a matter of being in the right place at the most opportune time. The lunar high should help you to take care of this and to reach a better understanding of what to do next. Everything now is about moving forward, and you probably won't take at all kindly to any sort of interruption.

23 WEDNESDAY   *Moon Age Day 7*   *Moon Sign Pisces*

If you have been fairly well occupied, you may have more or less forgotten that Christmas is just two days away. Use the power of the lunar high to get any remaining shopping done and to help you to find some bargains. Good luck may also on your side in other ways. Prepare to make last-minute changes work to your advantage.

24 THURSDAY   *Moon Age Day 8*   *Moon Sign Pisces*

The lunar high still lingers around you during Christmas Eve, which offers an extra boost in terms of energy and general happiness. You have what it takes to get things to drop into place at present and to give life the odd nudge in the right direction if necessary. Time alone with someone you love would be no bad thing this evening.

YOUR DAILY GUIDE TO DECEMBER 2009

25 FRIDAY *Moon Age Day 9   Moon Sign Aries*

You have potential to be at your happiest for Christmas Day if you surround yourself with people who are extremely important to you. Strangers take a back seat, even if you are out of the house and socialising. From a romantic point of view today could prove to be quite unique and some Pisceans could be in for a very special surprise.

26 SATURDAY *Moon Age Day 10   Moon Sign Aries*

Your lively, friendly attitude to the world at large means you may not be too keen to be trapped in the same place today – even if that is your own comfortable home. This would be an ideal time to visit relatives and to look out friends you don't get to see as much as you would wish. Stand by for a rollicking knees-up by the evening!

27 SUNDAY *Moon Age Day 11   Moon Sign Taurus*

You seem to get the very best from communicating today. This is because you have what it takes to modify your own nature for the sake of those around you. You can get even the most difficult of individuals to once again fall prey to your charm, and have what it takes to deal effectively with all practical matters. Don't forget to save time for your partner.

28 MONDAY *Moon Age Day 12   Moon Sign Taurus*

Any new social contacts you make should offer a marvellous tonic because just at the moment Pisces is as gregarious and sociable as it ever gets. Whilst others might get tired of the social whirl and demand a little rest, you can afford to dance on until dawn. If anyone can make the best of the Christmas holidays, you will probably be one of them.

29 TUESDAY *Moon Age Day 13   Moon Sign Taurus*

You have a talent for working hard and effectively, and can really show this now. Some Pisceans will be back at work and if you are one of them it's worth making certain that superiors know that you are around. There is nothing at all wrong with singing your own praises a little today, particularly if there is less competition around for the moment.

30 WEDNESDAY　　　*Moon Age Day 14*　*Moon Sign Gemini*

A fresh exchange of views should suit you fine today, and you needn't be at all insulted if someone wishes to modify one of your own notions. You are great when it comes to co-operation – even with people who have been difficult to deal with in the past. Niggling routines could get in the way of absolute enjoyment within your home.

31 THURSDAY　　　*Moon Age Day 15*　*Moon Sign Gemini*

New Year's Eve could not fall at a better time for you in an astrological sense. The position of Venus in particular assists you in large groups and ensures that your party spirit is still burning brightly. You have every reason to exit the year with a great sense of optimism. You also have exactly what it takes to be extremely helpful.

PISCES:
2010 DIARY PAGES

PISCES:
2010 IN BRIEF

The start of this particular year might be so busy it could be difficult for you to keep up with everything that is expected of you. January and February offer new opportunities to get on well in a professional sense, but the personal aspects are also favoured. There are possible gains on the financial front during February and you should also notice that your ability to influence the decisions others make is stronger.

March and April should bring you closer to achieving a desire that has been around for quite some time. Of course there will be ups and downs but the general feeling is one of progress and some satisfaction with your efforts. You might be slightly noisier than usual and more inclined to let people know exactly what you want from them. Avoid pointless routines at this time.

The early summer, May and June, should allow you to travel more and will offer new opportunities at work, as well as strengthening personal and romantic ties. You may feel at this time that you are approaching an important period at work or in some practical sense, and you certainly won't have any problems in your dealings with other people. This is when your intuition, which is always strong, begins to grow.

Look to July and August to further your interests in a financial sense and in terms of more distant travel. This might be holidays, but business trips are also possible. People you don't see too often could also figure in your life more fully around now and you will have energy available to do 'family things'. There is plenty to be done as far as work is concerned, but the main accent at this time is likely to be on fun and social situations.

September and October might be a time when you could expect things to slow down somewhat, except that this is not happening at all. You will be filled with energy, determined to keep moving forward and getting other people on your side. From a professional point of view you can really shine and there ought to be better financial possibilities showing themselves throughout both months.

The last two months of the year, November and December, should see you walking on air in a social and personal sense. These may be the best months of the year for love and there are gains coming along that you probably would not expect. Christmas is likely to be a family time as usual but there are indications that you will not relax the pace, even across the holidays. Pisces is scintillating as the year ends, and making a very good impression on everyone.

January 2010

1 FRIDAY   ☿   *Moon Age Day 16*   *Moon Sign Cancer*

Friendships receive the most positive planetary influences at this time. Joining forces with others could well prove very lucky, and there is much to be said for relying on the good offices of those around you. Ask yourself whether any slight niggles in the family are down to too much proximity across the Christmas holidays!

2 SATURDAY   ☿   *Moon Age Day 17*   *Moon Sign Cancer*

Beware of getting tied up with details today. Instead of looking at things through a microscope what you really need to do at present is to see the bigger picture. Creative potential is very well accented now, and you can use this to make things around you look good, even when it proves to be a rather difficult task.

3 SUNDAY   ☿   *Moon Age Day 18*   *Moon Sign Leo*

It's natural to want to get in touch with your inner self, and friends may well be able to help with that. At the same time this is an ideal day to make contact with useful people out there in the wider world. Communications over great distances are favoured during January, as is planning a long-term journey for later this year.

4 MONDAY   ☿   *Moon Age Day 19*   *Moon Sign Leo*

Some slight friction is possible today in your dealings with others, which is why choosing to go it alone in some situations would be no bad thing. When it comes to getting on with your lover you can ensure that there are no problems, and the same can be broadly true with people who have been close friends for a very long time.

YOUR DAILY GUIDE TO JANUARY 2010

5 TUESDAY ☿ *Moon Age Day 20 Moon Sign Virgo*

This is the start of the two-day period that comes along each month and is known as the lunar low. The Moon is in your opposite zodiac sign of Virgo, from where it supports a quieter interlude, potential irritations and a desire to get on quicker than seems to be possible. A little patience is the key, plus a greater reliance on other people.

6 WEDNESDAY ☿ *Moon Age Day 21 Moon Sign Virgo*

This won't be the best of days to make significant progress because the lunar low does little to help your efforts. Indeed it may seem that the harder you push, the greater is the resistance. This is where a little knowledge helps, because once you understand the lunar low you realise the best way to proceed is to let things flow around you.

7 THURSDAY ☿ *Moon Age Day 22 Moon Sign Libra*

With Mars in your solar sixth house it seems that being left to your own devices would be the ideal situation, particularly at work. Of course you can co-operate as well as usual, but you can be more efficient now when you do things alone. Be prepared to assist people who are seeking some good old-fashioned advice.

8 FRIDAY ☿ *Moon Age Day 23 Moon Sign Libra*

You should be able to attract support now from friends and colleagues. On the personal front, today would be ideal for reaching a new understanding with your lover or family members, and you can avoid rubbing others up the wrong way. With the weekend in view, why not plan something different and potentially exciting?

9 SATURDAY ☿ *Moon Age Day 24 Moon Sign Scorpio*

If you make sure your social diary is full, the weekend should offer many diversions from the normal pace of your life. Even if you are not particularly fond of the winter weather and the dark nights, you can find ways and means to make the sun shine indoors. On the other hand, you may decide to get well wrapped up and ignore the weather.

10 SUNDAY ☿ *Moon Age Day 25   Moon Sign Scorpio*

At work your argumentative side is emphasised, but of course many of you won't be at work on a Sunday. From a social point of view the trends are very different, and you have a chance to revel in the company of people you know well. Your ability to sort out any family problems, particularly concerning younger people, is highlighted now.

11 MONDAY ☿ *Moon Age Day 26   Moon Sign Sagittarius*

You are at your very best with professional developments and you have scope to win out right now when it comes to organising and inventing. Conforming to the expectations of others may not be easy, but you do have what it takes to disarm potential problems well before they get in the way of your overall progress.

12 TUESDAY ☿ *Moon Age Day 27   Moon Sign Sagittarius*

Teamwork and group activities could now begin to work better for you, and you should be at your best when you are co-operating, either at work or socially. This is a favourable time to seek new interests, and you shouldn't be stuck for ideas when it matters the most. Your ability to impress others counts for a great deal today

13 WEDNESDAY ☿ *Moon Age Day 28   Moon Sign Sagittarius*

Trends assist you to thrive in group situations or when associates or acquaintances are having a greater involvement in your life. Not everyone may be equally receptive to your charm, but keep trying because you have the ability to calm down even the most awkward people. You needn't be too hidebound by rules and regulations.

14 THURSDAY ☿ *Moon Age Day 29   Moon Sign Capricorn*

Positive friendships are once more underlined thanks to the present position of the Moon. It is towards people you have known for many years that you are now encouraged to turn for help and advice, and you are also in a good position to lend a hand to others if they need it. In a personal sense, acting on impulse is the name of the game.

YOUR DAILY GUIDE TO JANUARY 2010

15 FRIDAY ☿ *Moon Age Day 0   Moon Sign Capricorn*

There are signs that you could be taken to task over an issue within your work environment. You need to think quickly in order to resolve problems that have potential to get bigger than they need to be. Beware of giving in to negative thinking, because the more positive you remain in your attitude, the greater is the chance of progress.

16 SATURDAY ☿ *Moon Age Day 1   Moon Sign Aquarius*

Your strength lies in your willingness to take on board the opinions of those close to you, and you have an opportunity to learn a great deal about yourself by listening to what others are saying about you this weekend. If you don't always have a great deal of confidence, anything positive that sinks in can turn out to be very useful in the long run.

17 SUNDAY *Moon Age Day 2   Moon Sign Aquarius*

You work at your very best when you are co-operating, a fact that you can demonstrate throughout much of January. In any case it is the essence of Pisces to be approachable and to share. This is a Sunday that offers you the most if you ring the changes slightly. Forget the normal routines and let your hair down, perhaps with friends.

18 MONDAY *Moon Age Day 3   Moon Sign Aquarius*

A slightly quieter day is now on offer because the Moon is in your solar twelfth house. This influence supports a pensive time when you may be happy to watch and wait rather than to act. Impulsive behaviour is fine tomorrow, but for the moment it pays to clear the decks for action by getting half-finished jobs done and out of the way.

19 TUESDAY *Moon Age Day 4   Moon Sign Pisces*

Today is special because the Moon has now moved back into your own zodiac sign of Pisces, bringing the lunar high. Your general level of good luck is highlighted, as is your ability to know instinctively what you should do. Instead of letting negative types get in your way, you can afford to move forward at your own fast pace today.

YOUR DAILY GUIDE TO JANUARY 2010

20 WEDNESDAY   *Moon Age Day 5   Moon Sign Pisces*

The spotlight is on your ability to attract positive attention from others and to turn heads wherever you go. The middle of the week might not seem to be the best time to be pursuing a hectic social life, but that's what you have a chance to do. Lady Luck should be on your side, and there is much to be said for gambling just a little.

21 THURSDAY   *Moon Age Day 6   Moon Sign Aries*

It may be difficult now to be the main attraction because the Sun has moved into your solar twelfth house, encouraging you to concentrate on your personal life and your inner thoughts. After the last couple of days it might seem as though the brakes have been applied, but you should soon realise that it's worth quietening things down.

22 FRIDAY   *Moon Age Day 7   Moon Sign Aries*

In all competitive situations you can now be a very tough customer to beat. Even if you don't trumpet your abilities all over the place, in your quiet and solid way you have scope to make great progress and end up a real winner. Slow and steady wins the race, and this is truer for Pisces than for any other sign of the zodiac.

23 SATURDAY   *Moon Age Day 8   Moon Sign Aries*

There is a strong emphasis on communication, the expression of ideas and the need to make others fully conversant with your thinking. If there are people around who fail to listen to what you are saying, why not ignore them and move onto those who are happy to offer you an ear? It's time to look for excitement as far as your social life is concerned.

24 SUNDAY   *Moon Age Day 9   Moon Sign Taurus*

It is your love life that is under the spotlight under present trends. Pisces people who are in a settled relationship can ensure that harmony reigns, but if you are presently looking for love this should be a good time for keeping your eyes open. Instead of waiting for things to happen, it's a question of getting out there and jumping in the pool.

25 MONDAY
Moon Age Day 10   Moon Sign Taurus

The focus is on things that are going on at home that allow you to be busy, active and happy. Of course there could be slight niggles as well, like people who say one thing and do another, but you can get over these easily enough with your accommodating nature. You want to find the best in everyone right now and that is what happens.

26 TUESDAY
Moon Age Day 11   Moon Sign Gemini

Social matters can usually help you to get the very best from life, but especially so now that Mercury occupies your solar eleventh house. It gives you a chance to be noisier and to speak your mind, though in a way that others find disarming and charming. Looking attractive may not be hard, but you need to feel that way too!

27 WEDNESDAY
Moon Age Day 12   Moon Sign Gemini

Personal matters now offer the best rewards, and some of these could be quite surprising. It may be that things you did in the past are now starting to come good for you, and fortune smiles on you because of your previous generosity. Even if not everyone thinks you are flavour of the month, you can persuade enough people to like you.

28 THURSDAY
Moon Age Day 13   Moon Sign Cancer

When it comes to work situations you may decide that it's necessary to express your ego, even if you don't find this particularly comfortable. What you can't allow is for other people to walk all over you or to steal your ideas. You might have to be rather more forceful than you wish to be, but this is possible and sometimes essential.

29 FRIDAY
Moon Age Day 14   Moon Sign Cancer

Are you finding it difficult to elicit the appropriate response from your partner, or to get them to understand your point of view? You might have to work somewhat harder to get what you want today, or else realise that the time is not right for some things and wait a while before you concentrate your efforts again.

30 SATURDAY *Moon Age Day 15   Moon Sign Leo*

You have a chance to score great successes today, particularly if you know what you are talking about when other people do not. You can best keep ahead of the game by working hard but also by being willing to reap some of the benefits of your previous efforts. Be prepared to listen to what friends are saying, because some of it is good advice.

31 SUNDAY *Moon Age Day 16   Moon Sign Leo*

The emphasis is on your strong pioneering spirit at the moment, and this is linked to Mars, which presently occupies your solar sixth house. You can use your 'can do' attitude to help you reach your objectives, and you needn't allow minor irritations to get in the way. People should actively want to have you on their team at this time.

February 2010

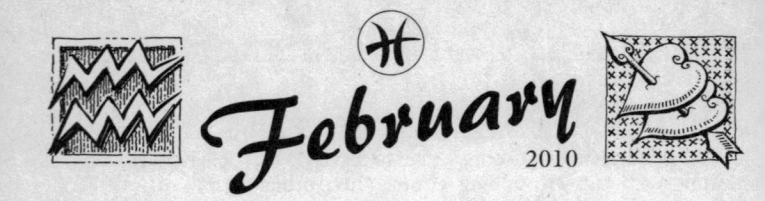

1 MONDAY
Moon Age Day 17   Moon Sign Virgo

There are good reasons to stick to tried and tested paths in the main as this week gets underway. Bear in mind that there are penalties for getting things wrong, and you will need to feel totally in charge of your own destiny. All things considered you should be proceeding rather carefully for the moment, but there is nothing too strange about that.

2 TUESDAY
Moon Age Day 18   Moon Sign Virgo

With the lunar low present you probably won't be pushing over any buses! If you are willing to rely on the good offices of colleagues and friends you can ensure that this slightly difficult phase passes without too many difficulties. It is only if you insist on going it alone no matter what that things may begin to get on top of you.

3 WEDNESDAY
Moon Age Day 19   Moon Sign Libra

You can afford to think of others as much as you consider yourself during this period. There's a danger of ending up at loggerheads with someone over issues that are not at all important. Ask yourself why you are being stubborn and unyielding, because once you have faced the question you should know how to disarm the situation.

4 THURSDAY
Moon Age Day 20   Moon Sign Libra

Despite the potential irritations of yesterday, there could be a sense today that you are just too accommodating for your own good. If you feel that people are taking you for granted, that isn't something you have to tolerate. One option is simply to withdraw your co-operation for a while to allow others the chance to think things through.

YOUR DAILY GUIDE TO FEBRUARY 2010

5 FRIDAY *Moon Age Day 21   Moon Sign Scorpio*

Trends suggest you may now be very susceptible to outside influences and to deceptions created by people who don't have your best interests at heart. You would be wise not to take anything for granted today, and it's worth checking all the details before making any binding commitments. Socially speaking you can be charming now.

6 SATURDAY *Moon Age Day 22   Moon Sign Scorpio*

If work relationships and partnerships now seem fraught with emotional difficulties, why not use this weekend as a welcome opportunity to do something quite different? Socially speaking it's a question of being on top form, willing to join in with just about anything and happy to mix and mingle with a broad cross-section of individuals.

7 SUNDAY *Moon Age Day 23   Moon Sign Scorpio*

Much of the present period offers you scope to make gains in your social life. You can ensure that discussions are positive, and you shouldn't go short of the right kind of attention from others. Spending too much time on your own isn't your best approach now. It is your associations with the world at large that now matter the most.

8 MONDAY *Moon Age Day 24   Moon Sign Sagittarius*

You should be able to get the maximum out of career matters at the moment and leave people in no doubt about your overall efficiency. With everything to play for in the personal stakes too, you are in a position to get a great deal out of life. If this isn't the case, you need to take a careful look to see what it might be that you are doing wrong!

9 TUESDAY *Moon Age Day 25   Moon Sign Sagittarius*

Much of your time today will be spent dealing with personal matters or situations that stand outside of your normal, everyday routines. There ought to be plenty to keep you occupied in a social sense and there isn't much doubt about the charm you show when in company. It looks as though everyone will want to have you around.

10 WEDNESDAY *Moon Age Day 26 Moon Sign Capricorn*

Personal attachments might be slightly in the doldrums today, and you may have to work that little bit harder in order to get on with certain people. If you have done your best but still can't get people to co-operate, be prepared to wait and see. It's time to give those around you space to move and think for themselves, even if to do so is hard.

11 THURSDAY *Moon Age Day 27 Moon Sign Capricorn*

Tensions at work are a distinct possibility, and you might need to re-examine work methods and relationships. Don't allow others to undermine your confidence, particularly if your own life is working out fine in general. As with yesterday, it might be necessary to let other people get on with being out of sorts – or even miserable.

12 FRIDAY *Moon Age Day 28 Moon Sign Aquarius*

Even if you can't make this the most rewarding of days at work, it shouldn't be long before you can turn things in your favour. For the moment you might have to concentrate on what you know to be important, whilst leaving other issues on the back burner. Socially speaking you have scope to improve things ahead of the weekend.

13 SATURDAY *Moon Age Day 29 Moon Sign Aquarius*

Difficulties are possible today if you don't make sure those around you are clear about what you are trying to say to them. Be unambiguous and don't allow any little misunderstandings to get in the way. There is a greater emphasis than ever on your ability to get your nearest and dearest to pitch on your behalf in a general sense.

14 SUNDAY *Moon Age Day 0 Moon Sign Aquarius*

If it looks as though your power and influence are on the wane today you can take heart in the knowledge that the lunar high is just around the corner. For the moment there is much to be said for relying on the good offices of friends. Today is also ideal for finding out whether you are quite as close to someone as you were in the recent past.

15 MONDAY
Moon Age Day 1   Moon Sign Pisces

Profit can now be gained through new initiatives and though a determination on your part to overcome any small obstacles that have developed in the last few days. Many of these might turn out to be paper tigers, because when you face them squarely they disappear altogether. Better times are available with regard to your personal life.

16 TUESDAY
Moon Age Day 2   Moon Sign Pisces

The continuing lunar high assists you to ensure that circumstances turn out very much as you would wish, and to get general good luck on your side during this part of the week. Be prepared to stick your neck out if you feel it is necessary. By all means take on board the opinions of others, though remember that it is your own that matter in the end.

17 WEDNESDAY
Moon Age Day 3   Moon Sign Aries

When it comes to work and professional matters generally you need to bear in mind the potential of your own temper. This is quite strange advice to be offering to the average Piscean subject, but with Mars now in your solar sixth house there are signs that you may be quicker than normal to take offence and to react.

18 THURSDAY
Moon Age Day 4   Moon Sign Aries

Your real forte at the moment is in the direction of personal attachments. The romantic side of the Pisces nature is legendary, and should be really working overtime just now. Your winning ways in a social sense are not in doubt either, and you can easily influence people and situations just by turning on that famous charm.

19 FRIDAY
Moon Age Day 5   Moon Sign Aries

Make the most of important discussions with influential people. You have greater scope to get what you want by being your most affable best and by showing just how much you care for those around you. Mixing work and play is the order of the day, and trends also support an almost irresistible urge to do some travelling.

20 SATURDAY *Moon Age Day 6   Moon Sign Taurus*

Making compromises could now be much easier than it was earlier in the month, assisting you to make this a fairly carefree and happy weekend. This is not a time to get upset about situations you can't alter, especially at home. Any tendency to show others that you are slightly unsure or hesitant is best avoided.

21 SUNDAY *Moon Age Day 7   Moon Sign Taurus*

Personal and professional matters are now well accented, with friendship high on your agenda and an ability to make firm friends from acquaintances. Almost anyone might fall prey to your charm at the moment, and that can give you a great deal of influence over others. Greater confidence to follow your own opinions should also be available.

22 MONDAY *Moon Age Day 8   Moon Sign Gemini*

A change for the better should be achievable in some relationships, especially those with people who have been hard to assess or deal with quite recently. Do you wish that you could spend more time alone with someone extra-special? There's nothing wrong with moving heaven and earth this week in order to make this a reality.

23 TUESDAY *Moon Age Day 9   Moon Sign Gemini*

Bear in mind that your present method of asserting yourself could get you into hot water, especially if you don't make sure that others understand what your motivations actually are. Getting on with work if there is a lot going on around you may not be exactly easy, but the best way forward is to take just one step at a time, and to go carefully!

24 WEDNESDAY *Moon Age Day 10   Moon Sign Cancer*

Trends place the emphasis on your ego today, and you may not be very easy to deal with in specific situations. The fact is that if you know how you want things to be done, you probably won't be too keen to alter your way of being on the say-so of others. Counting to ten now and again can help you to avoid arguments.

YOUR DAILY GUIDE TO FEBRUARY 2010

25 THURSDAY *Moon Age Day 11   Moon Sign Cancer*

The Sun has now entered your solar first house, supporting a strong sense of independence and a reluctance to do what you are told if you feel that whoever is telling you might be wrong. At the same time you have what it takes to display your confidence, and can use this to persuade people generally to follow your lead quite willingly.

26 FRIDAY *Moon Age Day 12   Moon Sign Cancer*

By all means keep to tried and tested paths at first today, but with the Sun in that fortunate position in your solar chart you should be able to achieve much of what you want around this time. You will have the ability to coerce others into following your wishes, and you might also have scope to score some significant successes in terms of love.

27 SATURDAY *Moon Age Day 13   Moon Sign Leo*

Keep busy and enjoy whatever is on offer this weekend. If you capitalise on new activities and situations that become available all around you there is no reason why you need to restrict your outlook. Today is also about taking the opportunity to lend a hand as far as others are concerned, and that might be what you love to do the most.

28 SUNDAY *Moon Age Day 14   Moon Sign Leo*

The end of the month is a chance to look forward to the upcoming spring and to get out of the house more than you have been doing during the coldest winter months. Things are beginning to wake up around you and this encourages a more adventurous attitude on your part. Make the most of the warmth you can attract from friends.

March 2010

1 MONDAY
Moon Age Day 15   Moon Sign Virgo

The lunar low comes along, encouraging you to be fairly steady in the way you approach this new week. There are gains to be made, though these are likely to be small in nature, and your finances are not particularly well accented. The spotlight is on the part that love plays in your life, and on the surprises it could bring.

2 TUESDAY
Moon Age Day 16   Moon Sign Virgo

Your best response to today is to find ways to enjoy yourself, but don't try to do too much. There are some ways of getting ahead, especially at work. The older the day grows, the more likely you are to be able to make progress. By the evening a chirpier outlook is possible, and you can ensure the lunar low is nothing more than an irritating memory.

3 WEDNESDAY
Moon Age Day 17   Moon Sign Libra

There is much to be said today for relying on the support of your friends, and possibly your colleagues at work. It isn't that you lack common sense, simply that there may be too many options around. Deciding what you are going to do under any given circumstances might not be easy, but you can work things out in the end.

4 THURSDAY
Moon Age Day 18   Moon Sign Libra

You can afford to be extra-persuasive when it comes to getting exactly what you want today, even if this is in stark contrast to what has been happening recently. It's time to take the initiative and to let everyone know that you are on the move. This would be an excellent time to travel or to plan for a lengthy journey you intend to take later in the year.

YOUR DAILY GUIDE TO MARCH 2010

5 FRIDAY
Moon Age Day 19   Moon Sign Scorpio

Socially speaking you should be ready to look far and wide in order to meet the right sort of people. This could mean that you decide to pursue new friendships, and is also an opportunity to get to know people who are already around you better than you did before. Even when there are distractions today, moving forward is still possible.

6 SATURDAY
Moon Age Day 20   Moon Sign Scorpio

If you use your skills to get people to understand what you mean, you can also persuade them to compromise. You can convince even the most awkward types to be more compliant, and people who scared you before should now seem like pussycats. It's about making full use of your own sweet and compliant nature, and your personal charm.

7 SUNDAY
Moon Age Day 21   Moon Sign Sagittarius

Are you encountering problems when are dealing with specific issues at home? One option would be to talk things through with someone older, wiser or both. Getting rid of small irritations should allow you to make the most of a day that responds to your wishes and ambitions. However, don't assume everything will turn out exactly as you expected.

8 MONDAY
Moon Age Day 22   Moon Sign Sagittarius

As communicative Mercury is now in your zodiac sign you can show what a quick thinker and an even quicker talker you can be. You needn't let people get the better of you when it comes to getting a message across, and you have what it takes to talk others into doing what you want. Small gains are also possible in a financial sense.

9 TUESDAY
Moon Age Day 23   Moon Sign Capricorn

You have scope to make this one of the best days of the month for potential gains of a material nature. Your energy, power and confidence are well accented, and you can ensure that nobody betters you in terms of your practical common sense. But even when you are go-getting you can still retain that innate Piscean sensitivity below the surface.

YOUR DAILY GUIDE TO MARCH 2010

10 WEDNESDAY *Moon Age Day 24   Moon Sign Capricorn*

Do remember that no matter how confident you are feeling at the moment there is only so much you can control at a practical level, and there might be occasions when you simply have to seek out the good offices of colleagues or friends. The time could be right to call in a few favours regarding some home-based issue or concern.

11 THURSDAY *Moon Age Day 25   Moon Sign Capricorn*

Avoid giving an untrustworthy impression by dithering over a vital issue. It would be better to make no comment than to jump about from foot to foot, and you certainly cannot afford to look in any way nervous today. Practical support should be there for the taking if you need it, and the advice you elicit from friends can make all the difference.

12 FRIDAY *Moon Age Day 26   Moon Sign Aquarius*

Financial matters now show greater potential for gains, and with the end of the week approaching you can also afford to leave some of the more practical aspects of life alone in favour of having some fun. Don't worry if something doesn't get done today. If it isn't vital, you might actually be able to achieve your objectives all the better later.

13 SATURDAY *Moon Age Day 27   Moon Sign Aquarius*

Trouble is best sidestepped now by adopting an amused attitude instead of losing your temper. This is particularly true in the case of issues that are quite definitely irritating but which you know are not going to last long. By all means give yourself a pat on the back for something practical you have achieved, but don't forget to set yourself a new target!

14 SUNDAY *Moon Age Day 28   Moon Sign Pisces*

This is one of the best days of the month for self-expression and for getting what you want simply because of the sort of person you are. The Moon has returned to your zodiac sign and joins the Sun there, offering a good time and plenty of good luck. You needn't sit in a corner at any stage today, because this is the time to shine.

YOUR DAILY GUIDE TO MARCH 2010

15 MONDAY *Moon Age Day 0 Moon Sign Pisces*

The impact you can have on others is now very noticeable, and you can use it to persuade people generally to follow your lead and to do you some favours. You are also in a position to get colleagues to sign up to your ideas and superiors to look at you very favourably. Be prepared to turn small gains early in the day into bigger ones later.

16 TUESDAY *Moon Age Day 1 Moon Sign Pisces*

If you have expensive tastes it looks as though now is the time to indulge them a little. There's nothing wrong with being up for the good life, and you can get more of what you want while the lunar high remains. Other planetary trends now support some laziness, so you need to make certain that you don't lounge around at all today.

17 WEDNESDAY *Moon Age Day 2 Moon Sign Aries*

Now is a time to gain greatly from fresh starts and innovations. It pays to take a more hands-on approach to practical matters, particularly if you think these won't work out half as well if you leave them to others. Your organisational skills are now second to none, and nobody knows better than you do right now what is good for your life.

18 THURSDAY *Moon Age Day 3 Moon Sign Aries*

Current trends favour information gathering, meetings and appointments. Today could also bring important news, possibly from far away, plus the chance for you to do some travelling of your own. Don't rest on your laurels just because something has started to come good for you. It's time to give the swing of life an even bigger push!

19 FRIDAY *Moon Age Day 4 Moon Sign Taurus*

A day to keep your eyes and ears open for news relating to important projects and to stay focused on issues you know instinctively to be important. Even if you discover that you have to look in several different directions at the same time, you needn't become distracted under present trends. The emphasis is on looking and feeling good.

YOUR DAILY GUIDE TO MARCH 2010

20 SATURDAY *Moon Age Day 5   Moon Sign Taurus*

Bear in mind that a negative atmosphere in your vicinity can have an adverse bearing on your own life, even if you are not directly involved. You would be wise to nip problems in the bud by talking to people and offering practical assistance before things get out of hand. A sensitive and calm approach works best with friends now.

21 SUNDAY *Moon Age Day 6   Moon Sign Taurus*

Domestic issues could take a turn for the better, offering you scope for happiness when at home today. At the same time you have planetary trends around you that infer movement, so sitting in a chair and reading a book is probably not the name of the game. The most profitable outcome might be to take a short trip with family members.

22 MONDAY *Moon Age Day 7   Moon Sign Gemini*

Monetary rewards can now be achieved, and they can arrive from some fairly surprising directions. You can also benefit from the actions of a partner and as a result of the good offices of your friends. Even if colleagues are slightly more difficult to deal with now, it still pays to get the measure of them.

23 TUESDAY *Moon Age Day 8   Moon Sign Gemini*

Practical projects are favoured around now, and it's time to show a renewed sense of urgency regarding a personal issue that you have let slip recently. Partnerships are especially well starred, and these could be of a personal or a practical sort. Even if you can get people generally to listen to what you have to say, will they act on your advice?

24 WEDNESDAY *Moon Age Day 9   Moon Sign Cancer*

It's OK to be a little self-absorbed at this stage of your life. With the Moon now in your solar fifth house it's worth trying to get some leisure and pleasure into your day, and there should be little reason to focus on anything you see as being sordid or dirty. This would be a great time to visit a health spa and to pamper yourself!

YOUR DAILY GUIDE TO MARCH 2010

25 THURSDAY   *Moon Age Day 10   Moon Sign Cancer*

The potential for acquiring money becomes greater, and you can reinforce this with your own changing attitude today. Make full use of the new ideas you have up your sleeve, and be prepared to share them with like-minded individuals. There are people around who know how to help you out, and you have scope to persuade them to do so.

26 FRIDAY   *Moon Age Day 11   Moon Sign Leo*

Capitalise on a potentially beneficial period as far as money is concerned. You might have plenty on your mind around now, but your practical skills are enhanced, and you shouldn't go short of accolades from other people. Your romantic life counts for a great deal now, and this would be an ideal time for Pisces subjects to start new relationships.

27 SATURDAY   *Moon Age Day 12   Moon Sign Leo*

It's natural to look at plans that are in the offing and assess whether they are more trouble than they are worth. However, analysing the situation carefully should allow you to find new ways to make things happen. An analytical approach to relationships is fine at the moment, but you need to avoid looking too deeply and with undue scepticism.

28 SUNDAY   *Moon Age Day 13   Moon Sign Virgo*

Patience is the key today when you are dealing with other people, but if anyone is capable of getting the best out of others it is you. Part of the problem now is the arrival of the lunar low, though you needn't let this trouble you unduly. With strong supporting planets and practicality from a second-house Sun, it's a question of soldiering on.

29 MONDAY   *Moon Age Day 14   Moon Sign Virgo*

It's possible that not all your plans will work out entirely as you would wish at the start of this week, and you might even have to think again completely about one issue. Ask yourself whether part of the problem is your own expectations of the behaviour of other people. It's time to use your skills of perception to the full, even with trivial matters.

30 TUESDAY
Moon Age Day 15   Moon Sign Libra

A fairly productive and fruitful phase is on offer, and with Mercury also now in your solar second house your ability to talk about practical situations knows no bounds. You shouldn't be dealing in pipedreams at this stage, and practically everything you think up has a common sense to it that you can get others to recognise immediately.

31 WEDNESDAY
Moon Age Day 16   Moon Sign Libra

Venus in your solar house of finance often suggests that a little good luck is available, but you can make even more progress if you remain astute and keep your eyes open around this time. You may even be able to make some gains as a result of taking small risks. True, these may well be very calculated, but this is not a time to hold back.

April 2010

1 THURSDAY   *Moon Age Day 17   Moon Sign Scorpio*

Today is about your willingness to be the main attraction as far as others are concerned and to communicate at every level. Conforming to the expectations of other people should be easy enough, but don't forget you have to please yourself too. Some of the demands being made of you might not be entirely fair or reasonable.

2 FRIDAY   *Moon Age Day 18   Moon Sign Scorpio*

You have a good potential for making money and the end of this particular working week should be plain sailing when it comes to business. The cultured side of your nature is emphasised, and you have what it takes to give a good impression when it really counts. Why not get dressed up tonight and find somewhere you can really shine?

3 SATURDAY   *Moon Age Day 19   Moon Sign Sagittarius*

Opportunities to get ahead lie in the information you gather today so it is important to keep your eyes and ears open. Don't wait for possibilities to arise, but instead, be prepared to force some issues when you know the outcome can be good. You are still very socially inclined and should be ready to mix and mingle with the best of them.

4 SUNDAY   *Moon Age Day 20   Moon Sign Sagittarius*

A day to put your best foot forward. Career prospects come under the spotlight under present trends, but you can afford to put these on one side for today and concentrate on enjoying yourself. Responding positively to the overtures of friends is the order of the day, and there is much to be said for joining them on a little Sunday adventure.

5 MONDAY
Moon Age Day 21   Moon Sign Sagittarius

Make the most of this chance to give your spirits a pleasant lift and to make an improvement of some sort in personal attachments. You know what you want and should have a very good idea how you are going to get it, and you can also persuade others to offer you assistance. This can be a very happy day for many Pisces subjects.

6 TUESDAY
Moon Age Day 22   Moon Sign Capricorn

The Sun is now in your solar second house and this assists you to seek out the finer things in life. As a Piscean individual you can get by on very little and your demands are few, but like everyone else you need to pamper yourself from time to time. You are in a position to capitalise on new social influences that are just beginning.

7 WEDNESDAY
Moon Age Day 23   Moon Sign Capricorn

Your energy levels are enhanced when it comes to practical matters, though you may be less inclined to push yourself in terms of your personal life. If you do have minutes or hours to yourself you could do worse than to spend at least some of these thinking deeply about various matters. Will outsiders recognise your present state?

8 THURSDAY
Moon Age Day 24   Moon Sign Aquarius

If you can manage to slow down the pace a little for today and tomorrow then so much the better. Whether we realise it or not, our whole lives respond to constantly changing cycles. For you at the moment the Moon in your solar twelfth house encourages you to take it steady, but in a couple of days everything is going to change.

9 FRIDAY
Moon Age Day 25   Moon Sign Aquarius

You have great strength when it comes to getting your message across to other people, though certainly not in a forceful or dominant manner. On the contrary, you have what it takes to be diplomatic and even a little calculating in your approaches, and that twelfth-house Moon is still in evidence, supporting a slightly subdued interlude.

YOUR DAILY GUIDE TO APRIL 2010

10 SATURDAY *Moon Age Day 26   Moon Sign Aquarius*

Even if you are still pensive at the start of today, you needn't allow this state of affairs to last very long. With every passing minute the Moon creeps closer and closer to Pisces, and it's natural to feel a great sense of anticipation and excitement. Why not get in touch with friends you don't see through the week and arrange something for later?

11 SUNDAY *Moon Age Day 27   Moon Sign Pisces*

This is definitely a day for going after what you want with all guns blazing. The lunar high enhances your confidence, and assists you to be insightful and even downright psychic. There is courage and optimism to spare, and a great desire to show the world what you can do. If things around you are quiet it will be up to you to pep them up.

12 MONDAY *Moon Age Day 28   Moon Sign Pisces*

By all means focus your sights on money-making efforts and go for gold at work. New opportunities and responsibilities could well be on offer, and you have no reason to turn away from either right now. An ideal day for improving your personal resources and for thinking up new ways to get ahead of the crowd and to stand out.

13 TUESDAY *Moon Age Day 29   Moon Sign Aries*

Today offers you scope to create interesting social events and new happenings that should pep up your life and make you feel more excited about the future. This would be an excellent time to take a journey, even if it is one inside your head – for the moment at least. Planning is something you can do at present without even realising.

14 WEDNESDAY *Moon Age Day 0   Moon Sign Aries*

It's natural to get impatient if your ideas and schemes don't work out quite as quickly as you may have hoped. Try to be patient and don't force issues, especially in personal relationships. It's a question of giving those around you time to respond to your overtures because constantly trying to convince them could be counterproductive.

15 THURSDAY *Moon Age Day 1   Moon Sign Taurus*

Making agreements and deals with colleagues should be well within your capabilities at the moment, and you are easily able to get your own way with just a little ingenuity and persuasion. This is an especially favourable interlude for getting on well with workmates, particularly if you make sure they understand your point of view.

16 FRIDAY *Moon Age Day 2   Moon Sign Taurus*

Communication matters are still on a roll, though there could be a slight element of indecisiveness to be dealt with at some stage today. Trends suggest you may have arrived at some sort of crossroads, and it now remains for you to decide which path to take for the future. It pays to seek out a little wise advice from someone you really trust.

17 SATURDAY *Moon Age Day 3   Moon Sign Taurus*

Be ready to focus on personal needs and matters closely connected with your home today. This may not be too difficult at the weekend, but you also need to be prepared to move and to act at a moment's notice in order to avoid missing out on important opportunities. You have scope to make life exciting around this time.

18 SUNDAY ☿ *Moon Age Day 4   Moon Sign Gemini*

There could be a real sense of urgency about getting things done and this is partly linked to the present position of Mars in your solar sixth house. This supports a slightly impatient interlude, and might incline you to snap at others if they won't keep up your speed. Don't overreact to setbacks and take little problems in your stride.

19 MONDAY ☿ *Moon Age Day 5   Moon Sign Gemini*

Take advantage of the chance to make yourself the centre of attention. After all, there's nothing wrong with wanting to be adored by others, particularly as you aren't often in this frame of mind. In reality it shouldn't be hard for you to get the attention you crave if you are willing to show people how adorable you really are.

20 TUESDAY ☿ *Moon Age Day 6 Moon Sign Cancer*

It's true that you like to be liked but this, after all, is a normal human desire. As a Pisces subject you may well spend a great percentage of your life working for and on behalf of others, so it isn't at all unfair to have the world looking after your needs once in a while. It's time to turn on the charm and wait for others to respond.

21 WEDNESDAY ☿ *Moon Age Day 7 Moon Sign Cancer*

Your strength now lies in your willingness to seek alternative methods of getting ahead in a professional sense. It takes initiative and inventiveness to get exactly what you want, but since you have plenty of both you can make this a very positive period. Your ability to gain attention from various directions continues to count for a great deal.

22 THURSDAY ☿ *Moon Age Day 8 Moon Sign Leo*

Current trends favour pet projects, particularly ones related to work and health. Today is about making the most of a peak in energy and sorting out once and for all any little trials and tribulations that you have carried from the past. Bear in mind that conforming to the social expectations of others might not be as easy as you thought.

23 FRIDAY ☿ *Moon Age Day 9 Moon Sign Leo*

Diplomacy rules, but since this is your middle name it needn't be an issue for the average Pisces subject. All the same, if dealing with younger family members seems like treading on eggshells, some care will be necessary. The trouble is that it may be difficult to second guess the way they are likely to react between now and Sunday.

24 SATURDAY ☿ *Moon Age Day 10 Moon Sign Virgo*

Stand by to deal with the lunar low, which has potential to affect your weekend somewhat if you don't take the right sort of actions. Instead of trying to push ahead rapidly, you need to be more circumspect and to be willing to watch and wait. Patience is also the best way to respond to any rules and regulations that get on your nerves.

YOUR DAILY GUIDE TO APRIL 2010

25 SUNDAY ☿ *Moon Age Day 11   Moon Sign Virgo*

There are good reasons to let your partner or someone else in the family handle things, while you take some time out to do whatever takes your fancy. You may not want to travel too far today, though short journeys could be enlivening and might take you out of yourself. Don't be surprised if you are more easily upset than usual around this time.

26 MONDAY ☿ *Moon Age Day 12   Moon Sign Libra*

Opportunities present themselves today for you to communicate fully with others, even those you haven't had much to do with in the recent past. You now have what it takes to elicit a more positive reception from these individuals, and to persuade any reticent friends to toe a more reasonable line.

27 TUESDAY ☿ *Moon Age Day 13   Moon Sign Libra*

There could be some pause for thought as far as romance is concerned, and you need to consider whether you are happy with how things are going in this area of your life. Remember that there may be nothing seriously wrong, and you could be getting matters out of proportion. It's worth getting awkward jobs out of the way early.

28 WEDNESDAY ☿ *Moon Age Day 14   Moon Sign Scorpio*

You can get new projects up and running quickly and efficiently, so much so that you may not realise just how effective you are being. Your strength lies in your ability to get the best out of colleagues and friends, even if family members are still creating slight difficulties. Why not spend some free time with friends, and have a good laugh?

29 THURSDAY ☿ *Moon Age Day 15   Moon Sign Scorpio*

This is a time for expansion. The Moon is now in exactly the right position to give you a leg up the ladder of life, and there could be new opportunities for advancement at work or in a social sense. Something you haven't been looking forward to might actually turn out much better than you expected, and you can afford to revel in good company.

30 FRIDAY

Moon Age Day 16   Moon Sign Scorpio

There are certain choices that have an element of good luck about them, even if you don't recognise this immediately. Although there might also be specific setbacks to deal with, you are in a position to sort these out immediately and before they can cause you any real trouble. You should be looking and working ahead of yourself.

May 2010

1 SATURDAY   ☿ *Moon Age Day 17*   *Moon Sign Sagittarius*

Getting what you want from life shouldn't be too difficult this weekend, though you might have to pause to give someone in the family some more support. It's natural to get annoyed it people don't take your advice on board, especially if that puts them in a situation that is even harder to deal with.

2 SUNDAY   ☿ *Moon Age Day 18*   *Moon Sign Sagittarius*

Don't be afraid to put personal issues on the shelf as you respond to demands from the outside world. By the time you go back to look at them they may have either shrunk or disappeared altogether. It's amazing how situations can sort themselves out, and in any case you should be able to find plenty of people at the moment that you can call on.

3 MONDAY   ☿ *Moon Age Day 19*   *Moon Sign Capricorn*

By thinking smart instead of simply working hard you can achieve all sorts today. Optimism and positive thinking are great assets to you at the moment and you shouldn't go short of praise either – which is always a psychological help. Your enthusiasm is your best friend, and it's a pity that you don't have it with you always.

4 TUESDAY   ☿ *Moon Age Day 20*   *Moon Sign Capricorn*

Domestic matters could now be more fulfilling than can sometimes be the case, and you have potential to get a great deal out of even the most mundane of chores. Perhaps it is simply a case of enjoying a good job well done, though it might also be down to your capacity to think up newer, better and more efficient ways to deal with drudgery.

YOUR DAILY GUIDE TO MAY 2010

5 WEDNESDAY ☿ *Moon Age Day 21*   *Moon Sign Aquarius*

Trends suggest that material progress today might not be quite as easy as it has been, and there is much to be said for being a little careful regarding your spending. By all means be generous to those you care for, though it pays to hold onto cash if you think people are trying to rip you off. Are there ways you could cut down your domestic expenditure?

6 THURSDAY ☿ *Moon Age Day 22*   *Moon Sign Aquarius*

This could well be a fairly taxing time in a professional sense, and you need to be prepared if little things are going wrong on a regular basis. Your best response is to laugh at these situations if you can and simply move along at your own speed and with your confidence untroubled. This is certainly not a time to allow panic to creep in.

7 FRIDAY ☿ *Moon Age Day 23*   *Moon Sign Aquarius*

'One step at a time' is the right adage for Pisces today, especially since the Moon is in your solar twelfth house, supporting a contemplative and quieter interlude. In personal attachments a fairly inventive approach would be no bad thing, particularly if ordinary responses haven't had the impact you wish. A day to seek attention from friends.

8 SATURDAY ☿ *Moon Age Day 24*   *Moon Sign Pisces*

Greater self-confidence and vitality are the gifts of the lunar high, which coincides absolutely with the weekend this month. If you set out to enjoy yourself, you have what it takes to make it happen. Change and diversity is the key, so don't be afraid to get out of the house and do something completely different – and perhaps slightly mad!

9 SUNDAY ☿ *Moon Age Day 25*   *Moon Sign Pisces*

This is a time when your powers are at their very best. You should be quite happy to stretch yourself today and can afford to seek new horizons at every turn. There is an underlying element of good fortune in almost everything you do, and you can use your heightened powers of discrimination now to make all the right choices.

10 MONDAY ☿ *Moon Age Day 26   Moon Sign Aries*

Keep abreast of major news and views and make sure that you pay attention to those you know to be knowledgeable. You could do much worse than to join forces with powerful individuals at this time, and if you decide to harness yourself to their sleigh you stand a chance of making far more progress than you possibly could on your own.

11 TUESDAY ☿ *Moon Age Day 27   Moon Sign Aries*

Today is about how willing you are to keep on the go, and there is no reason to slacken your pace much throughout this particular Tuesday. Bear in mind that if you are busy, there's a chance you will forget an anniversary of some sort, and that might lead to a little unpopularity. Why not check the calendar today before you get started?

12 WEDNESDAY ☿ *Moon Age Day 28   Moon Sign Aries*

You have scope to make this a fairly relaxed time, which you will probably need if you've been busy across the last few days. The Moon is in your solar third house, so a chatty and generally cheerful approach still works best. An easy manner is the order of the day, and it allows you scope to increase your popularity.

13 THURSDAY *Moon Age Day 29   Moon Sign Taurus*

Planetary changes taking place now show that there is much to be gained from your home and the people in it across the next few days. Venus is now in your solar fourth house, assisting you to get ever closer to those to whom you are related, but especially to your partner. You might decide that new individuals should play slightly less of a role just now.

14 FRIDAY *Moon Age Day 0   Moon Sign Taurus*

You needn't react too harshly to any apparent let-downs at work. Bear in mind that these could well be minor in nature and quite recoverable. Concentrate today on keeping the wheels of progress turning effectively and efficiently. Do friends seem complicated under present trends? Be prepared to use your intuition in order to understand them.

15 SATURDAY   *Moon Age Day 1   Moon Sign Gemini*

Communication is the keynote to ultimate success at this time. There is much to be gained from what you hear when you are out and about, so it really is worth keeping your ears open at the moment. Use what you know to good advantage and pass on information immediately if you know it will be useful to colleagues or friends.

16 SUNDAY   *Moon Age Day 2   Moon Sign Gemini*

Today would be ideal for catching up on correspondence, even if you are also busy in a social sense. The year is advancing and there is much to be said for spending time out of doors, appreciating the turning seasons and gaining from a little fresh air. You might decide to take others with you. There is genuine joy to be found in relationships now.

17 MONDAY   *Moon Age Day 3   Moon Sign Cancer*

Capitalise on favourable social conditions and the opportunity to show off a little. There is no reason at all why you should hide your light under a bushel, especially when you have so much to offer. Romance is well accented, and you should be in a position to make the most of it. You may even have an admirer you didn't suspect.

18 TUESDAY   *Moon Age Day 4   Moon Sign Cancer*

Take advantage of the chance to adopt a leadership role at work. Even if this comes about because nobody else wants the task, you can soon demonstrate how dedicated and efficient you can be. If your work involves caring for others you have what it takes to be ultra-efficient, but the compassion of all Pisces subjects is highlighted now.

19 WEDNESDAY   *Moon Age Day 5   Moon Sign Leo*

All family matters have potential to be pleasurable under present trends, and you shouldn't have any difficulty when it comes to entertaining people, either inside or outside your home. Being the centre of attention is a natural aspect of life now, despite the fact that this position isn't always comfortable.

20 THURSDAY *Moon Age Day 6   Moon Sign Leo*

A day to follow through on recent proposals regarding work. The emphasis is on organising yourself and letting others know exactly what you are doing. By all means seek help if you need it, though there could be many situations in which you are quite happy to go it alone. There's nothing wrong with being quieter than usual.

21 FRIDAY *Moon Age Day 7   Moon Sign Virgo*

With the lunar low arriving you might feel it would not be wise to try to shine in public situations for the next few days. On the contrary, you could be more comfortable creeping into your own little cave and waiting there in the dark. However, there are also positive planetary positions around, so be prepared to stay out there!

22 SATURDAY *Moon Age Day 8   Moon Sign Virgo*

Although today could be fairly low key, there are still ways in which you can get ahead. The lunar low is a time for planning rather than doing, but this is a necessary process and one that stands you in good stead later on. Even entertaining is possible today, though you might decide to limit such activities to your own home.

23 SUNDAY *Moon Age Day 9   Moon Sign Virgo*

There are good reasons to put family matters high on your personal agenda at this time and to focus on domestic issues as much as proves to be possible. This might mean you are not quite as available to friends as usual, and you need to ensure you don't stretch your abilities too far – at least until tomorrow's trends come along.

24 MONDAY *Moon Age Day 10   Moon Sign Libra*

If you have to abandon something and start again, so much the better. There are definite gains to be made right now from being willing to reorganise and retrench. The lunar low is now well out of the way and the trends generally favour a more direct and dominant approach. At the same time, the magnetic side of your nature is highlighted.

25 TUESDAY
Moon Age Day 11   Moon Sign Libra

Trends support a deep need right now to make yourself heard, especially in practical situations and when you are at work. The spotlight is on your instinctive sense of how things will turn out, and this can guide you if you decide to make a bet of any kind. This trait can be especially useful if you apply it to the behaviour of friends.

26 WEDNESDAY
Moon Age Day 12   Moon Sign Scorpio

If it feels as though there is something missing today, your best approach is to try to discover what it might be. It's natural to worry that you are not being included in secrets, but you need to consider that there may be little or nothing to know. All the same, you can't always cry 'coincidence', because conspiracies do sometimes exist.

27 THURSDAY
Moon Age Day 13   Moon Sign Scorpio

Career plans now receive definite and practical planetary assistance. Before making any moves it's worth carefully considering all the options. There is also an opportunity at this time to meet people who are strangers now but who could become increasingly important to your life in the weeks and months ahead.

28 FRIDAY
Moon Age Day 14   Moon Sign Sagittarius

This is a day when you can score points with just the force of your own personality. Romance and love affairs look especially well marked, and it pays to be prepared to respond to surprises, particularly later in the day. You can afford to concentrate at least some of your efforts on getting family members to do what you know is best for them.

29 SATURDAY
Moon Age Day 15   Moon Sign Sagittarius

Enjoying family relationships may prove even easier at this time, and you seem to have what it takes to make everyone feel good about their own abilities. Giving support to others allows you to increase your popularity, and possibly even attract a few accolades! This is a weekend during which fun should play an important part.

30 SUNDAY
Moon Age Day 16   Moon Sign Capricorn

New planetary influences assist you to strengthen your resolve and get what you want from life. This includes finding new ways to express yourself, something that can really make a difference today. Seeking out new groups or organisations would suit the present astrological scene, and could be a chance to prove your abilities as a leader.

31 MONDAY
Moon Age Day 17   Moon Sign Capricorn

The focus is on your willingness to meet challenges head-on, and this week offers you the chance to shine in both professional and social settings. Things should be coming together, especially in terms of friendship, and you have scope to demonstrate your practical side. By all means stand up for yourself if you feel your rights are being infringed.

June 2010

1 TUESDAY
Moon Age Day 18   Moon Sign Capricorn

On the first day of June you may well have to use some fairly subtle tactics in order to get your own way. You don't always appreciate your own ability to work out how others are likely to behave under any given circumstance. At the moment this trait is more notable than ever – verging on the extraordinary in some cases!

2 WEDNESDAY
Moon Age Day 19   Moon Sign Aquarius

Trends encourage you to be on the move, and your curiosity knows no bounds. Even if there is plenty to get done, you have what it takes to do it effortlessly and with a cheerful attitude. Make the most of this interlude by completing any jobs that have been tedious, and finish them with as much enthusiasm as you had when you began.

3 THURSDAY
Moon Age Day 20   Moon Sign Aquarius

Have you been leaving a particularly awkward job until last? The funny thing is, it may now seem easy to complete. Although a slightly quieter approach works best today, you can still plan, because the real energy and enthusiasm will be called for from tomorrow. Set the scene for fascinating social encounters, and perhaps a journey.

4 FRIDAY
Moon Age Day 21   Moon Sign Pisces

It is the professional part of your life that should benefit the most from the arrival of the lunar high, though it has to be said you can be on fine form in every respect and more than willing to put yourself out for others. Lady Luck is with you and helps you to make the right decisions. You can ensure that money matters now look better than of late.

YOUR DAILY GUIDE TO JUNE 2010

5 SATURDAY *Moon Age Day 22   Moon Sign Pisces*

Today you needn't go short of friendly help and assistance. It's a question of calling the shots and using the influence you have over life. It might surprise you how willing others are to do what you think is right, and this could extends to usually awkward types. In most respects you can make this one of the smoothest days of the month.

6 SUNDAY *Moon Age Day 23   Moon Sign Pisces*

You would be wise to proceed with caution today, but only in so far as your professional life is concerned. There are signs that not everyone is exactly what they appear to be. In other respects the day can be positive, and might offer you the chance to get away from mundane situations. Create excitement for yourself and your friends.

7 MONDAY *Moon Age Day 24   Moon Sign Aries*

Now is the time to concentrate more on developments in your love life and also to think hard about romantic journeys you might want to make soon. Even if matters of the heart are working out more or less as expected, you would be wise to be extra vigilant when it comes to remembering anniversaries. This is a day to pay attention.

8 TUESDAY *Moon Age Day 25   Moon Sign Aries*

You can now achieve a shift of emphasis in terms of your sense of security, and make life slightly more settled and comfortable as a result. Your finances and everyday working conditions are well marked for the moment, and this would be an ideal time to seek out people who might be in a position to do you some extra good this week.

9 WEDNESDAY *Moon Age Day 26   Moon Sign Taurus*

Be prepared to make use of any ingenious ideas you have up your sleeve now, and with the Moon in your solar third house you will also be in a good position to address emotional and romantic matters. A slightly more nostalgic interlude than usual is indicated, but there is nothing especially odd about this for Pisces.

YOUR DAILY GUIDE TO JUNE 2010

10 THURSDAY *Moon Age Day 27   Moon Sign Taurus*

If you take care in your dealings with others you should be able to deal with any tensions that are around at the moment. Even if these aren't being created by you, you might have to respond to someone's frustration. Defusing situations is something you are very good at, so be ready to prove it today.

11 FRIDAY *Moon Age Day 28   Moon Sign Gemini*

Make the most of your current self-confidence and your appreciation of what is needed for you to score some significant successes, especially at work. The spotlight is on future plans and career objectives, and on your ability to influence the decisions of your partner to a greater extent than seems to have been the case.

12 SATURDAY *Moon Age Day 0   Moon Sign Gemini*

All love life and leisure issues receive positive planetary highlights right now because Venus is occupying your solar fifth house. When Venus is in this position you have scope to make lovely things happen, and you should be in a very receptive frame of mind as far as emotions are concerned. New love is possible for some Pisceans at present.

13 SUNDAY *Moon Age Day 1   Moon Sign Gemini*

Family situations can be the source of significant rewards, and you may be able to derive some benefit from accolades achieved by those around you. There is also an emphasis on travel, or at the very least working out the details of journeys you intend to take in the not too distant future. Above all, your optimism should be there for all to see.

14 MONDAY *Moon Age Day 2   Moon Sign Cancer*

You may now decide to withdraw from the world a little more than was the case during the last week or so. This isn't too surprising because the Sun is in your solar fourth house, as is little Mercury. These trends highlight the importance of your own home and personal surroundings, so it would be no surprise if outside situations seemed threatening.

YOUR DAILY GUIDE TO JUNE 2010

15 TUESDAY
Moon Age Day 3   Moon Sign Cancer

Practical ideas and planning should now begin to take centre stage again, and with Venus moving into your solar sixth house you can afford to be more confident in your approach to life in a general sense. Today offers you scope to gain recognition for past actions, and to accept positions of responsibility offered by others.

16 WEDNESDAY
Moon Age Day 4   Moon Sign Leo

In a work sense you now have what it takes to get things into much better focus. This is a potentially productive time and you need to seize opportunities as they present themselves. Do you feel responsible for others? Although that might add a small load to your mind from time to time, this is nothing you cannot deal with easily.

17 THURSDAY
Moon Age Day 5   Moon Sign Leo

With everything to play for in a social sense you are in a position to be the life and soul of any party that is taking place. It is worth pursuing these trends right now because for a day or two a quieter and somewhat more reclusive interlude prevails. It's time to let people know how you feel about them, and even to whisper words of love!

18 FRIDAY
Moon Age Day 6   Moon Sign Virgo

There might be little scope for personal or ego triumphs whilst the lunar low is around, and in any case you may not be too interested in competing today or tomorrow. On the contrary, there is much to be said for simply sitting and cogitating about things. You needn't become a hermit, but your own company should suit you well enough.

19 SATURDAY
Moon Age Day 7   Moon Sign Virgo

This is a day to keep life as uncomplicated as proves to be possible. Be prepared to respond to pressure, and to seek the support of family members in order to deal with something that might give you no problems as a rule. Later in the day you should be able to get more or less back to your earlier form and ready to seek excitement.

YOUR DAILY GUIDE TO JUNE 2010

20 SUNDAY *Moon Age Day 8   Moon Sign Libra*

Trends assist you not only to get along with others at this time but also to benefit from such encounters. Now you can really turn life to your advantage, particularly if you can mix and mingle with the sort of people who are in the best position to give you a leg up of some sort. Romance also looks well marked, and remains so next week.

21 MONDAY *Moon Age Day 9   Moon Sign Libra*

Reducing the amount of time you spend at work this week would be no bad thing, especially if this gives you more hours to pursue your own interests and to be with family members. In particular, it's a question of getting yourself in tune with the needs of your partner, so it pays to be in their company as much as possible.

22 TUESDAY *Moon Age Day 10   Moon Sign Scorpio*

The more variety you can bring into your life around now, the better you should feel. What you probably don't need is to be stuck in situations you find tedious or boring. A day to search out some excitement and stay as much as possible in the company of people you find stimulating. New ideas could well be available all the time now.

23 WEDNESDAY *Moon Age Day 11   Moon Sign Scorpio*

There are signs that you might be rather full of yourself in the immediate future, and this is linked to the present position of the Sun in your solar chart. No matter how arrogant you think you are becoming, you can avoid upsetting anyone else because it isn't in your nature to be overbearing. All it really means is that you are confident.

24 THURSDAY *Moon Age Day 12   Moon Sign Sagittarius*

Even if you are now keeping up a high profile as far as your work is concerned, it is family bonds that could be the most significant component of your life at this time. There are good reasons to plan ahead for a family-motivated weekend and also to get together with anyone who you feel has been somewhat ignored in the recent past.

25 FRIDAY *Moon Age Day 13   Moon Sign Sagittarius*

This has potential to be a dynamic and inspiring period in professional terms, and this influence is linked to the position of Moon, which is now in your solar tenth house. Make the most of the chance to reap the results of efforts you have put in previously, and to come to terms at least with any issues that have bothered you a while.

26 SATURDAY *Moon Age Day 14   Moon Sign Sagittarius*

It's time to capitalise on potentially happy trends that are operating in your life generally, and to ensure you are satisfied with the way things are going. The weekend offers you the chance to do something quite different and you could be quite lucky at this time. A shopping spree in the company of a good friend might suit you very well.

27 SUNDAY *Moon Age Day 15   Moon Sign Capricorn*

If personal relationships are slightly less harmonious now than you think they should be, perhaps you need to find out why this is the case. Is someone harbouring a grudge or feeling aggrieved about something that is unknown to you? The best way to find out the truth is to ask a few searching questions.

28 MONDAY *Moon Age Day 16   Moon Sign Capricorn*

Your strength now lies in your ability to make an impact on the world at large. The Sun is in a positive position for you, and general trends are favourable for most of the coming week. Rather than getting involved in pointless arguments today, your best approach is to find ways and means to be friends with as many people as possible.

29 TUESDAY *Moon Age Day 17   Moon Sign Aquarius*

You have scope to make this a fun day, in the midst of a period in which the charming side of your nature is to the fore. Trends encourage a light-hearted approach and a willingness to offer just the right sort of advice to others when it is most needed. With little to hold you back, this could also be one of the most lucrative periods of the month.

30 WEDNESDAY   *Moon Age Day 18*   *Moon Sign Aquarius*

There are signs that a relationship matter could take the wind out of your sails, especially if you are not expecting it. The focus is now on your ability to deal with powerful feelings, both on your own behalf and with regard to those around you. Be prepared to respond to any friends who are in need of your special support.

July 2010

1 THURSDAY
Moon Age Day 19   Moon Sign Aquarius

The start of a new month also coincides with the approach of the lunar high. Even if today starts out fairly quiet, that's not the way things need to stay for many Pisces subjects. On the contrary, life has potential to get busier and busier, though not in a way you should find difficult. Putting in some extra effort can make all the difference.

2 FRIDAY
Moon Age Day 20   Moon Sign Pisces

This is a day on which it should be easy to step out into the spotlight and to get what you really want. You can afford to feel very confident, particularly if in most situations you know very well what you are talking about. Lady Luck plays an important part in the events of today, so be ready to push yourself forward at every opportunity.

3 SATURDAY
Moon Age Day 21   Moon Sign Pisces

This is a time for taking risks and for rolling the dice in the certain knowledge that the result will be what you seek. Pisces can be quite shy and retiring, but this needn't be the case right now. Particularly favourable and rewarding trends are on offer this week for those who care for others in the professional sphere.

4 SUNDAY
Moon Age Day 22   Moon Sign Aries

Today offers you scope to ensure your work is in harmony with the rest of your life, an important fact for Pisces. You hate things to be in any way out of balance and you are happiest when life is one continuum. The results of something you did recently could now be coming in. Did you do better than expected?

5 MONDAY
Moon Age Day 23   Moon Sign Aries

Now the emphasis is firmly on fun. You rarely take yourself too seriously, and at the moment you can be more carefree than ever. Why not get cracking and see how your personality can make a big hit with everyone? Of course there will be some people around who refuse to be amused by anything, but you can do your best to ignore them.

6 TUESDAY
Moon Age Day 24   Moon Sign Aries

Today works best if you remain on the move and are focused on getting things done from morning until night. This applies not only to how busy you are at work but also to what you can accomplish at home. Confidence should be easy to find, and you can respond positively to the professional and personal expectations that others have of you.

7 WEDNESDAY
Moon Age Day 25   Moon Sign Taurus

Venus is in your sixth house, which is favourable for working closely with others. You should be able to modify your own nature to suit that of those around you, and although this is a skill you always possess it is much accentuated at the moment. You should be able to tap into professional help today if you find you need it.

8 THURSDAY
Moon Age Day 26   Moon Sign Taurus

Favourable influences come through love and leisure activities at this time. This is a period when you will be happy to be in the limelight and keen to pursue the accolades that are due to you. Personal attachments that mean so much to you can become even more significant and special under the present position of the Sun.

9 FRIDAY
Moon Age Day 27   Moon Sign Gemini

If a personal relationship needs more attention, it might bring some unexpected pressures. In the main you should be able to get life ticking along nicely, though you will have to be careful not to spread yourself around so much that nothing gets done properly. Today is a chance to show everyone the extent of your popularity.

10 SATURDAY
Moon Age Day 28   Moon Sign Gemini

Whilst professional interests will continue to be of paramount importance, the weekend could well offer its own interests that are far from any work-based matter. This would be an ideal time to deal with details that have been waiting all week, and also to spend a few hours in the company of relatives you wish to catch up with.

11 SUNDAY
Moon Age Day 29   Moon Sign Cancer

Social life and friendships come under the planetary spotlight today. Capitalise on the chance to get romantic issues working in your favour and to make yourself flavour of the month in someone's book. Trends indicate the possibility of a gift, probably as a result of something you did ages ago, or else comments that are as good as a present.

12 MONDAY
Moon Age Day 0   Moon Sign Cancer

Take advantage of promising romantic developments. At the moment you have what it takes to really knock people off their feet, and your magnetic personality is likely to be of use in a number of different situations. If this is the start of the working week for you, today is about making the sort of impression that lasts for days.

13 TUESDAY
Moon Age Day 1   Moon Sign Leo

You need to make yourself aware of any small but significant communication difficulties that exist between yourself and other people. Ask yourself whether you are failing to get your message across to a specific individual, or whether it's the case that they don't want to hear what you are saying. Patience is always your way forward.

14 WEDNESDAY
Moon Age Day 2   Moon Sign Leo

The Moon is now in your solar sixth house and quite often this assists you to create favourable work conditions and beneficial communications with colleagues and superiors. Now is the time to ask for a raise if you have been thinking about this for a while, and you can also absorb more responsibility without really thinking about it.

YOUR DAILY GUIDE TO JULY 2010

15 THURSDAY *Moon Age Day 3   Moon Sign Virgo*

As the lunar low arrives, you might have to contend with taxing situations, particularly in a professional sense, though under present trends this is something you can take very much in your stride. It's worth keeping your ambitions reasonable and within defined bounds, but at the same time you needn't be too modest!

16 FRIDAY *Moon Age Day 4   Moon Sign Virgo*

With the lunar low still around this is not the best period in which to push yourself too hard, nor to take the sort of risks that have been par for the course at other times so far this month. It would be better to show your moderate side and to allow the good advice of those who care for you to sink in for a few hours.

17 SATURDAY *Moon Age Day 5   Moon Sign Libra*

Today marks a time to make room for creative impulses to have their head. You need to do your own thing and to be yourself, no matter what you are up to and no matter who you are with. People should find your nature refreshing and your present candid approach very much to their liking. Bear in mind that there will always be exceptions.

18 SUNDAY *Moon Age Day 6   Moon Sign Libra*

You should now have little trouble getting your own way in personal relationships, and some Pisces subjects could even see new romance blossoming at this time. Rather than being over-modest when the compliments come in, you need to recognise that to some people you are really important. It's great to know what others think of you.

19 MONDAY *Moon Age Day 7   Moon Sign Scorpio*

Variety and diversity are what you are all about, and with the summer weather present you can afford to get out of doors and enjoy what nature has to offer. Travel should be well highlighted and if you have chosen this period to take a holiday you could hardly have picked a better time. Make the most of an interlude when the planets are on your side.

20 TUESDAY *Moon Age Day 8   Moon Sign Scorpio*

Be prepared to deal with testing times around now, particularly within personal attachments. These are linked to the present position of the planet Mars. Are you finding the behaviour of those close to you difficult to understand? Modifying your own nature may be the best way of dealing with such situations.

21 WEDNESDAY *Moon Age Day 9   Moon Sign Sagittarius*

This could be an excellent time to get out and about and to meet others. Even if you don't already know the people in question, you can ensure you soon do, and you have scope to make new friends at any time now. Increasing your social circle significantly is part of what present planetary trends are all about. Creating a good atmosphere is the key.

22 THURSDAY *Moon Age Day 10   Moon Sign Sagittarius*

Trends in the workplace look favourable, and you have what it takes to start something new alongside colleagues or friends. If your love life isn't going exactly to plan this may be related to the planet Mars, which does little to assist your efforts at this time. In the main you should be able to cope with any issues that do arise.

23 FRIDAY *Moon Age Day 11   Moon Sign Sagittarius*

You have what it takes to ensure that what is happening around you is plain sailing and filled with a sense of entertainment and fun. Beware of taking on too much in a practical sense that is new. It's not that you can't deal with it, but that you might have so much to do in your social and love life that there simply won't be enough time!

24 SATURDAY *Moon Age Day 12   Moon Sign Capricorn*

There are gains to be made from social engagements around now and from mixing and mingling with people from a variety of different backgrounds. It pays to be just a little careful when it comes to getting your own way. Remember that a little extra tact can make all the difference if you are dealing with awkward types.

YOUR DAILY GUIDE TO JULY 2010

25 SUNDAY *Moon Age Day 13   Moon Sign Capricorn*

Competition of any sort is well starred on this particular Sunday, and there is much to be said for getting involved in new sporting activities or else showing how good you are at what you already enjoy. Although winning can be important to you it isn't the most important factor. Pisces does genuinely like to take part.

26 MONDAY *Moon Age Day 14   Moon Sign Aquarius*

Potential romantic promise is around for most of the coming week and you can also use this interlude to boost your popularity in a general sense. You might not believe that you exude sex appeal, but you need to ask yourself what other people think. It isn't just your looks or your figure. It is Pisces people's wonderful natures that really shine.

27 TUESDAY *Moon Age Day 15   Moon Sign Aquarius*

Be careful that you don't overlook minor but nevertheless important details in the workplace. Trends support a slightly absent-minded interlude in which you may not be quite as efficient as usual. There may also be a tendency to seek a retreat of some sort and to sit in it! It's natural for Pisces to need these periods of reflection sometimes.

28 WEDNESDAY *Moon Age Day 16   Moon Sign Aquarius*

In another day or so the lunar high will come along, encouraging you to feel better about yourself and more confident of your own abilities. For the moment there is much to be said for relying on what others can do for you, and this probably isn't the best possible day to seek advancement or to show your skills.

29 THURSDAY *Moon Age Day 17   Moon Sign Pisces*

Good fortune is there for the taking, and you have what it takes to get things working in your favour while the Moon remains in your zodiac sign. You can afford to take a few more chances than you have been doing for the last few days and to rid yourself of any tendency to hesitate. Showing Pisces at its best is the order of the day!

30 FRIDAY
Moon Age Day 18   Moon Sign Pisces

There is a strong impetus for new projects and a feeling that you can get life to follow the path you wish. Most of what you achieve is down to your own confidence and your determination to make a splash. Even if people actively want to have you around, you may not be any more popular today than you usually are.

31 SATURDAY
Moon Age Day 19   Moon Sign Aries

This has potential to be another exciting period as far as leisure and romantic matters are concerned, though instead of the lunar high this is linked to the present position of Venus in your solar chart. A word in the right ear could work wonders this weekend, and all you really need to do is to work out whose ear this should be.

August 2010

1 SUNDAY
Moon Age Day 20   Moon Sign Aries

The greatest benefits today can be gleaned through communication with other people, especially individuals you know are on your side to begin with. Be prepared to fill your social diary and to put yourself in the market for travel, no matter how far it might be. You might even take yourself by surprise when it comes to arrangements.

2 MONDAY
Moon Age Day 21   Moon Sign Aries

It's time to get down to business, especially when you are at work. There are new starts to be made and opportunities available that you never suspected. It pays to be ready for these, so clear the decks for action and get yourself motivated. Outside of work you can afford to be up for more challenges and a dose of excitement.

3 TUESDAY
Moon Age Day 22   Moon Sign Taurus

You can now ensure that your love life is operating in a very comfortable way and that your popularity is strong. Socially speaking this is an ideal time to put yourself at the very centre of other people's arrangements, and you may have to act on the spur of the moment in order to avoid disappointing someone. A day to listen to friends.

4 WEDNESDAY
Moon Age Day 23   Moon Sign Taurus

It's natural for rules and regulations of one sort of another to get on your nerves at the present time, because you really just want to do what appeals to you. Trends emphasise the mischievous side of your nature at the moment, and this could prompt some impish and slightly erratic behaviour. If this doesn't sound like Pisces – it isn't!

5 THURSDAY   *Moon Age Day 24*   *Moon Sign Gemini*

You may need to impose a greater degree of discipline on yourself when it comes to work. You might still be something of a loose cannon, so won't be too inclined to do the expected thing. Give yourself time to be the individual that you are and don't flog yourself for not being exactly 'normal' at the moment. You can soon change things.

6 FRIDAY   *Moon Age Day 25*   *Moon Sign Gemini*

Relationships can now be given a little more sparkle, and with Mercury in your solar seventh house you are encouraged to be chatty and to make the most of opportunities to pick up on useful information that is available. Does it seem that other people are playing games with you today? You should be wise and astute enough to deal with that.

7 SATURDAY   *Moon Age Day 26*   *Moon Sign Cancer*

Your ability to command attention has rarely been better and your tendency to impress people should be put to good use today. Instead of asking yourself whether you should be doing certain things, why not get on and do them? Once you have finished you can look back and marvel at what you are capable of achieving when you pitch in.

8 SUNDAY   *Moon Age Day 27*   *Moon Sign Cancer*

Your emotional life could be even better at this time, and you needn't be backward at coming forward when in company. It's time to show that you are good to have around, and to recognise how much you are appreciated by others. Outdoor activities are the order of the day, so find some space to breathe.

9 MONDAY   *Moon Age Day 28*   *Moon Sign Leo*

Don't be surprised if you don't feel particularly secure today. Mars is in your solar eighth house and from this position it supports a somewhat edgy interlude, even though this can be a very positive planetary position. You can now overthrow past difficulties and embark upon adventures that would have seemed like a dream just a short time ago.

10 TUESDAY
Moon Age Day 0   Moon Sign Leo

There's nothing wrong with analysing yourself and others at the moment. It can be a useful process, though there might be occasions when you are looking too deeply. In some situations your best approach is to accept what life is offering and to take other people's word for their honesty and sincerity. Trust your intuition to guide you.

11 WEDNESDAY
Moon Age Day 1   Moon Sign Virgo

The lunar low has arrived, and for some Pisces subjects it is inclined to take the wind out of your sails, especially where your physical condition is concerned. Feelings of fatigue and stress are possible, even if you are not pushing yourself too hard. The response is quite simple: take some time out and have a rest.

12 THURSDAY
Moon Age Day 2   Moon Sign Virgo

There is much to be said for keeping a low profile at the moment and for not expecting too much of yourself. It will be possible to seek support from those around you, particularly if you are only calling in favours that other people owe you. Make the most of more positive influences on the financial front.

13 FRIDAY
Moon Age Day 3   Moon Sign Libra

Mars is still in its eighth-house position, giving you the impetus you need to consider letting go of something that is no longer of any use to you. There could be a degree of nostalgia involved, but you will have to be slightly tough on yourself for your own future good. At home, involving younger people in your plans can work wonders.

14 SATURDAY
Moon Age Day 4   Moon Sign Libra

You now have scope to make new acquaintances, and to turn some of these into important friends in the weeks and months ahead. If you haven't already met your soul mate, you may have a good chance to do so quite soon. However, this is unlikely to happen unless you get yourself out there into the wider world and look around.

15 SUNDAY
Moon Age Day 5   Moon Sign Libra

There is now an emphasis on the attention you give to your inner mind and the thoughts that are occupying you at this time. If serious issues arise, bear in mind that in the fullness of time you might realise that these are nothing of the sort. This is one day during August when it is essential not to take yourself too seriously.

16 MONDAY
Moon Age Day 6   Moon Sign Scorpio

The freedom-loving side of your nature is now highlighted, and you probably won't appreciate being held back in any way. You need an intellectually challenging stimulus and should revel in puzzles or quizzes of any sort. Travel is well starred, and on the way you have a chance to learn as much as you can about an increasingly fascinating world.

17 TUESDAY
Moon Age Day 7   Moon Sign Scorpio

When it comes to relating at a personal level it is possible that many demands are now being made of you. You needn't allow these to have too much of a bearing on you, and in the main you should be quite willing to comply with the wishes of those you love. At home there is no reason whatsoever why harmony should not prevail today.

18 WEDNESDAY
Moon Age Day 8   Moon Sign Sagittarius

You now have a great ability to sense the right time for any particular action, and what's more, you have the knack of putting yourself in the right place. You can do yourself a great deal of good by pushing situations more and by showing a willingness to modify your stance when necessary. Pisces can be a quick learner at the moment.

19 THURSDAY
Moon Age Day 9   Moon Sign Sagittarius

Make the most of the chance to accrue benefits in the money department. Some of these might be as a result of your past actions, but there is also a possibility that you can tap into an enhanced level of good luck. Even if you aren't much of a gambler as a rule, taking more chances is a natural aspect of life at this time.

20 FRIDAY
Moon Age Day 10   Moon Sign Capricorn

Your ability to get social relationships working well is to the fore, and this would be an ideal day to mix with the sort of people who have it in their power to do you some good. There are good reasons to move your attention away from personal ambitions and towards efforts to help the people around you.

21 SATURDAY
☿ *Moon Age Day 11   Moon Sign Capricorn*

This has potential to be an emotionally restless sort of day and one that will work out better if you keep on the move. You needn't give yourself too much time to sit and ponder over situations because you can sort these out to your advantage by simply remaining patient. This would be a great day for a shopping spree, perhaps with friends.

22 SUNDAY
☿ *Moon Age Day 12   Moon Sign Capricorn*

Although you may be quite idealistic in terms of the way you look at romance right now, you have what it takes to get things working out very much the way you wish. If you are willing to remain confident about the actions of others, they shouldn't let you down. This can be a delightful Sunday for many sons and daughters of Pisces.

23 MONDAY
☿ *Moon Age Day 13   Moon Sign Aquarius*

You have the capacity to be very understanding and sympathetic. There is nothing remotely unusual about this because you are, after all, a Pisces subject. What might be different is that you are demonstrating to more people what a kind and helpful person you are. As a result, you could be receiving accolades you didn't seek and don't expect.

24 TUESDAY
☿ *Moon Age Day 14   Moon Sign Aquarius*

In general there is more intimacy and understanding on offer at the moment. Relationships can be consolidated and you can afford to push your luck a little with friends, especially if there is something you want from them at the present time. It pays to be bold at work, even with superiors, because a little cheek can go a long way now.

YOUR DAILY GUIDE TO AUGUST 2010

25 WEDNESDAY ☿ *Moon Age Day 15 Moon Sign Pisces*

You are now at your most persuasive and you can get almost anything you want by simply asking in the right way. The lunar high adds to your confidence and assists you to make the very best impression on other people. It's a question of ensuring you are on top form both physically and mentally, and refusing to dwell on things too much.

26 THURSDAY ☿ *Moon Age Day 16 Moon Sign Pisces*

At this time you can clearly define what you want to achieve and your level of general good luck is much higher than usual. It's time to go for gold, both in sporting activities and with regard to life in general. Make space for personal enjoyment, and if it is at all possible, travel to somewhere interesting and stimulating right now.

27 FRIDAY ☿ *Moon Age Day 17 Moon Sign Pisces*

You might have to slightly reassess what you want from life, though you should be able to do it in a very positive way. Not everything you planned for this year might have worked out quite as you would have wished, and now is the time to put that right. It is truly amazing how much personal power you now have at your disposal.

28 SATURDAY ☿ *Moon Age Day 18 Moon Sign Aries*

Relationships can now benefit from a very positive planetary boost, and you have the ability to be extremely effective when it comes to getting others involved in your life. At a personal level you have what it takes to make someone special take notice of you, and should also be demonstrating to the world just how personally positive you can be.

29 SUNDAY ☿ *Moon Age Day 19 Moon Sign Aries*

Emotional attachments now offer scope for great rewards, and even if you have been very busy across the last few days you are now in a good position to take time out to show people how important they are to you. An air of contentment should be following you around today, and if it is not, you are probably doing something wrong.

YOUR DAILY GUIDE TO AUGUST 2010

30 MONDAY *Moon Age Day 20   Moon Sign Taurus*

Be prepared to deal with possible conflict situations today, and beware of overplaying your hand when it comes to disputes at work. Remember that if you let people know everything they will be in a better position to get one over on you. There is much to be said for staying as quiet as a mouse when your instincts tell you to do so.

31 TUESDAY *Moon Age Day 21   Moon Sign Taurus*

The Moon is now in your solar third house, a position from which it helps you to unearth new information that could be quite useful to you in the days and weeks ahead. You can plan successfully at this time, and you may already be on the move because travel is favoured for a period around the end of this month.

September 2010

1 WEDNESDAY ☿ *Moon Age Day 22   Moon Sign Gemini*

You can now ensure that professional developments are positively influenced by happier conditions in your home environment. You can do much to improve your living conditions, even if you are not the sort of person who wishes to live in a palace. It's more about finding ways of making other family members feel more comfortable.

2 THURSDAY ☿ *Moon Age Day 23   Moon Sign Gemini*

Trends indicate there may be no stopping you today, and wherever you go you can create an air of anticipation and excitement. The positive responses this helps you to attract from others can do a great deal to boost your own optimism. It's a favourable time, and you need to be right on the ball to fully appreciate it.

3 FRIDAY ☿ *Moon Age Day 24   Moon Sign Cancer*

Emotions are on the up, and your ego is as big as it ever gets! You can use your present power to make a good impression on just about anyone, and the timorous side of Pisces may be nowhere to be seen. Make the most of these positive trends by doing something different and by demonstrating your silly and funny side.

4 SATURDAY ☿ *Moon Age Day 25   Moon Sign Cancer*

Partnerships and personal relationships are where the benefits now lie, and the weekend should offer you plenty of chance to find happiness at a deeply personal level. This doesn't mean you have to moon around. On the contrary, it's time to be bright and vivacious, and to make the most of the fact that the planets are smiling on you.

5 SUNDAY ☿ *Moon Age Day 26 Moon Sign Leo*

This has potential to be a highly favourable period for personal advancement, especially in the case of Pisces subjects who work at the weekend. Even if you don't, there are ways and means of getting ahead. Rather than waiting around in any crowd, it pays to push your way gently to the front and show people that you know what you are talking about.

6 MONDAY ☿ *Moon Age Day 27 Moon Sign Leo*

This is a time when you should be thinking about strengthening the bonds between yourself and others, especially in a personal and romantic sense. You could also have a chance to tap into monetary assistance, maybe from fairly surprising directions. The spotlight is on your willingness to put in some work out there in the community this week.

7 TUESDAY ☿ *Moon Age Day 28 Moon Sign Leo*

If you have plenty to do and can capitalise on the incentives on offer, you can make this a fairly rewarding day. However, the lunar low is just around the corner so it might be worth tying up any loose ends before the potentially quieter and less energetic phase arrives. You needn't get flustered today by rules, even pointless ones.

8 WEDNESDAY ☿ *Moon Age Day 0 Moon Sign Virgo*

Be prepared to hang fire with any important decisions. The lunar low could well slow things down and make it difficult for you to arrive at the proper conclusions. It's natural to want to retreat into your own little shell, particularly if you find it difficult to deal with other people. Bear in mind that these are all very temporary concerns.

9 THURSDAY ☿ *Moon Age Day 1 Moon Sign Virgo*

A lack of emotional understanding is unusual for you, though it's certainly possible today. Ask yourself whether you are failing to take on board the wishes of your partner or family. Remember that this needn't last for long, because by this evening the lunar low has moved away. Why not spend time later in the day with loved ones?

YOUR DAILY GUIDE TO SEPTEMBER 2010

10 FRIDAY ☿ *Moon Age Day 2 Moon Sign Libra*

Today is about being well versed in a social sense and about showing the fact now that the Sun is in your solar seventh house. Getting together with others should be meat and drink to you, and this would be an ideal time to mix with people who are brand new to your life. Be prepared to offer your expertise in a number of different ways.

11 SATURDAY ☿ *Moon Age Day 3 Moon Sign Libra*

You can benefit from being on the move and from exploring new territory. It doesn't matter whether this is geographical or mental – what is important is your willingness to get on with life. You may well have a great deal to say in company, which contrasts with the more retiring side of your nature. Make the most of your current popularity.

12 SUNDAY ☿ *Moon Age Day 4 Moon Sign Scorpio*

Does it feel as if someone is testing your patience in an emotional sense? You have the instinctively ability to know what to abandon and what will work if you keep trying. Although it may be difficult to be quite as accommodating as might sometimes be the case, there's nothing to stop you swapping ideas with bright people.

13 MONDAY ☿ *Moon Age Day 5 Moon Sign Scorpio*

You now have scope to gain from communications with newcomers into your life and to stretch yourself as much as possible, especially when it comes to your intelligence. The emphasis is also on the humorous and witty side of your nature, and on using this to seek success in a social sense. Don't be surprised if everyone wants to know you.

14 TUESDAY *Moon Age Day 6 Moon Sign Sagittarius*

This remains a favourable time to be alongside colleagues and to work co-operatively in every sphere of your life. Even if not everyone is equally easy to deal with, you can afford to show great persistence in order to bring people round to your point of view. Be prepared to put the finishing touches to a long project.

YOUR DAILY GUIDE TO SEPTEMBER 2010

15 WEDNESDAY *Moon Age Day 7   Moon Sign Sagittarius*

This has potential to be another positive day for co-operative ventures and it's all down to the present position of the Sun. People don't always instinctively follow your lead, but you have what it takes to persuade them to do so now. This is an ideal time to start new incentives and to push your luck a little, especially at work.

16 THURSDAY *Moon Age Day 8   Moon Sign Capricorn*

Your social life and friendships can be given the support they need, probably with minimal effort. The focus is on getting most areas of life running quite smoothly and on your determination to get what you want as far as your love life is concerned. Bear in mind that displaying a positive approach could dissuade others from arguing with you.

17 FRIDAY *Moon Age Day 9   Moon Sign Capricorn*

Your talent for communicating ideas is well starred, and you can make full use of your diplomatic skills under most circumstances today. Defusing situations is something at which you excel at the best of times, but right now you could be working for the United Nations! It's a question of modifying your own stance to suit others.

18 SATURDAY *Moon Age Day 10   Moon Sign Capricorn*

Your eagerness to please everyone is emphasised today, though of course this is an impossible task! Be prepared to concentrate on people who will listen to you, and stay away from argumentative types altogether. Even the most awkward individuals might come round if you give them time, and there is no gain at all today from arguments.

19 SUNDAY *Moon Age Day 11   Moon Sign Aquarius*

It's time to be inspired by wide horizons and by new opportunities, even ones that are far into the future. You can afford to look at life in a long-term sense and shouldn't be quite as impatient with yourself or circumstances as you may have been recently. Look for opportunities to make small financial gains today and turn these to your advantage.

20 MONDAY
Moon Age Day 12   Moon Sign Aquarius

Beware, Pisces, because trends at the moment encourage a tendency to go against the general consensus that exists around you. It would be easy to fall in line and in some ways more beneficial. However, if that's not the way you are feeling, you need to be prepared for some major discussions and even arguments today.

21 TUESDAY
Moon Age Day 13   Moon Sign Pisces

The Moon returns to your zodiac sign, assisting you to feel on top of the world. Whether all that many people will want to be there with you remains to be seen, particularly if you allow the bossy side of your nature to prevail. At least you are in a position to get what you want from life and to use the general good luck that is on offer.

22 WEDNESDAY
Moon Age Day 14   Moon Sign Pisces

This is a time for inspiration and activity. In many respects you can make it the best part of the month, and it offers you all sorts of fantastic incentives for now and the future. It would be a shame to ignore any of these, but of course you are only one person and there is a limit to what you can get done in a single day.

23 THURSDAY
Moon Age Day 15   Moon Sign Pisces

Even if the business of the day is overtaken by events you didn't expect, the presence of the lunar high allows you to deal with these instinctively and in a very positive way. By all means give yourself a pat on the back for something you have achieved this week, but don't rest on your laurels because there is probably still plenty to be done.

24 FRIDAY
Moon Age Day 16   Moon Sign Aries

Long-distance travel and contact with people from other cultures could well appeal to you. Certainly such matters are favoured by the astrological picture as it stands, and you can choose to make the most of these trends or ignore them. A day to make sure you are on top form when it comes to mixing with people you find particularly stimulating.

25 SATURDAY *Moon Age Day 17   Moon Sign Aries*

Your sense of self-importance tends to be bound up with your opinions right now, and it could be that in some ways you are not behaving like the archetypical Pisces subject at all. It is all too easy for you to get on your high horse, and you probably won't be inclined to stand any nonsense. Woe betide anyone who pushes you into a corner!

26 SUNDAY *Moon Age Day 18   Moon Sign Taurus*

You have scope to benefit from a wide range of interests right now. It's time to be mentally sharp, easy to deal with and definite about what you want. Your strength lies in your ability to get on with others, though they may sense that your nature runs much deeper than it appears on the surface. Of course they would be correct.

27 MONDAY *Moon Age Day 19   Moon Sign Taurus*

This is a period during which your driving force is strong and you can continue to take the world around you and mould it into the shape you require. It is unusual for Pisces to go through such protracted positive periods, but it does assist you to get what you want for more of the time. You can afford to feel satisfied with your performance.

28 TUESDAY *Moon Age Day 20   Moon Sign Taurus*

There are trends about that encourage a convivial and light-hearted approach, and these are very important when it comes to your social life. There is no immediate sign of the positive planetary influences coming to an end, so if you feel that you yourself are running out of steam, you would be wise to pace yourself regarding certain issues.

29 WEDNESDAY *Moon Age Day 21   Moon Sign Gemini*

Mars is in your solar ninth house, which is adding to the assertive spell you currently have at your disposal. In most situations you should know when you are right and you needn't brook any interference once you have made up your mind. There are gains to be made on the financial front, even if some of them come as a surprise.

30 THURSDAY — Moon Age Day 22 — Moon Sign Gemini

The spotlight is on your strong motivation and your desire to investigate the world at the most minute level. A careful, tidy and ordered approach is the name of the game, especially in your work. Be ready to capitalise on some interesting social invitations that could lead to even more fascinating possibilities later.

October 2010

1 FRIDAY
Moon Age Day 23   Moon Sign Cancer

This would be a favourable time for getting together with like-minded people in order to discuss any matters that have been on your mind. Do you find yourself rushing towards the end of projects just so that you can start on new ones? Bear in mind that you could exhaust yourself as a result. Getting some genuine rest can work wonders.

2 SATURDAY
Moon Age Day 24   Moon Sign Cancer

You have what it takes to come up with good ideas for joint financial enterprises. Today offers scope to start new projects, perhaps with friends, who may also become business partners in some cases. Your love life might have been slightly ignored in the recent past, but that phase is now coming to an end. It's time to show your devotion.

3 SUNDAY
Moon Age Day 25   Moon Sign Leo

This has potential to be a good time for keeping up the general progress that has been a hallmark of your life for the last week or two. Sunday should also offer a little more time to take a rest, but even then you could have things on your mind. Activity is meat and drink to you, and you shouldn't have any difficulty understanding others.

4 MONDAY
Moon Age Day 26   Moon Sign Leo

Monetary complications are a distinct possibility around now, and you may need to organise some fairly serious discussions with family members. It pays to scrutinise cash flow carefully and to avoid spending on unnecessary luxuries this week. It would be far better to pile up the coins, at least until around the middle of the month.

5 TUESDAY
Moon Age Day 27   Moon Sign Virgo

Getting ahead in a general sense could prove somewhat problematic whilst the lunar low is around. Be prepared to rely more heavily on the advice and help of your friends, because even if your judgement is not seriously impaired it might be difficult to see things as clearly as would normally be the case.

6 WEDNESDAY
Moon Age Day 28   Moon Sign Virgo

This is unlikely to be the luckiest day of the month as far as you are concerned, so unnecessary speculation is best avoided at this time. By all means keep yourself busy, but not so much so that you end up being tired all day. What really matters is keeping your mind occupied and focusing on situations that are due to mature later this month.

7 THURSDAY
Moon Age Day 29   Moon Sign Libra

A new period of inspiration is on offer around now. This can assist you to bring interest and renewal into your professional life and put a spring in your step as far as romance and socialising are concerned. Although some people think about hibernation as the autumn weather closes in, you have scope to enjoy the season.

8 FRIDAY
Moon Age Day 0   Moon Sign Libra

This is a favourable time for intimate relationships and a period when you can afford to show your sympathy for anyone who is having difficulties. It's fine to look to the past for inspiration regarding current issues, though you shouldn't allow nostalgia to get in the way of your decision making. Keep an eye on situations that are maturing at work.

9 SATURDAY
Moon Age Day 1   Moon Sign Scorpio

You have what it takes to be a fairly quick-thinking person, even if it sometimes takes you a while to act. Today the speed of your responses is emphasised, assisting you to make gains simply by being in the right place and acting instinctively. This could be especially true in terms of money, which you can pursue more easily now.

YOUR DAILY GUIDE TO OCTOBER 2010

10 SUNDAY   *Moon Age Day 2   Moon Sign Scorpio*

Bear in mind that your judgements in some directions could well be affected by changes taking place in your environment. Meanwhile, travel is well accented, and you may even decide to take the journey of a lifetime – either now or in the not too distant future. This is an ideal time for family discussions and family decisions.

11 MONDAY   *Moon Age Day 3   Moon Sign Sagittarius*

Don't avoid necessary change and be willing to adjust your opinions to accommodate altering circumstances. You can't afford to be a creature of habit at the moment and will get the most out of life if you move about and refuse to get stuck in a particular way of thinking. The more flexible you are, the greater the rewards you can achieve.

12 TUESDAY   *Moon Age Day 4   Moon Sign Sagittarius*

In a professional sense there may be many tests around at this stage of the week. It could be that bosses want to know what you are capable of doing, and if you remain positive you should be able to give a good account of yourself. There is little point in worrying about your love life, even if there are a few hiccups just now.

13 WEDNESDAY   *Moon Age Day 5   Moon Sign Sagittarius*

Make the most of a potentially inspiring sort of day. The Moon is in your solar eleventh house and social issues especially are well marked. It's time to get out and about and to consolidate your popularity among friends. There is a focus on communication, so get ready to respond if messages do come in around now.

14 THURSDAY   *Moon Age Day 6   Moon Sign Capricorn*

Though communication matters still have much going for them at this time, you might run the risk of spoiling things by being over-zealous in your ideas. It's important to keep a sense of proportion and to avoid getting too involved in situations that could be rather dubious. Stay away from anyone who appears to be just too smooth.

YOUR DAILY GUIDE TO OCTOBER 2010

15 FRIDAY *Moon Age Day 7   Moon Sign Capricorn*

Today is a chance to examine certain parts of your life, particularly relationships, and to decide whether they are working out exactly as you had hoped. Even if it appears things are fine, you may be given to pointless worrying right now, something you should try to avoid. Don't hold on so tight – you will enjoy the ride more!

16 SATURDAY *Moon Age Day 8   Moon Sign Aquarius*

Today is a favourable time for broadening your horizons, and there is much to be said for trying something new and finding talents you didn't know you possessed. On the other side of the coin, today might not work out so well if you plod along the same line you usually follow at the weekend. Some fresh air can make all the difference.

17 SUNDAY *Moon Age Day 9   Moon Sign Aquarius*

Practical affairs might not be running as smoothly as you would wish, and you need to be ready to deal with any potential setbacks. Some of these could be blessings in disguise, because they offer you a chance to look at situations in a different light and try out new strategies. What you can't afford to do at the moment is to stand still.

18 MONDAY *Moon Age Day 10   Moon Sign Aquarius*

This is the last day prior to the lunar high, which can certainly give you a shot in the arm this month. For today you need to be thinking about finishing things off and getting your stall set out for new projects and unusual ideas. By all means have fun and take advantage of the social invitations that are on offer now.

19 TUESDAY *Moon Age Day 11   Moon Sign Pisces*

The lunar high presents new opportunities when it comes to furthering your aims and getting your life on track. You can use the actions of those around you to pave the way towards your own little successes, and co-operation is an important keyword at the moment. You needn't get obsessed with rules and regulations. For now you can make your own!

YOUR DAILY GUIDE TO OCTOBER 2010

20 WEDNESDAY *Moon Age Day 12   Moon Sign Pisces*

Personal choices and self-determination are key factors when it comes to your happiness at this stage of the month. Be prepared to take a chance or two and also be willing to rely on the good offices of anyone your intuition tells you is trustworthy. You are now about as adventurous as Pisces gets – which should prove exciting.

21 THURSDAY *Moon Age Day 13   Moon Sign Aries*

When it comes to work there needs to be an element of risk about right now – that is if you are to get as much from life as is possible. Sitting and counting your pennies might be rewarding in one way, but if you want to make the pile grow you will have to do something positive. Socially speaking you can now remain on top form.

22 FRIDAY *Moon Age Day 14   Moon Sign Aries*

It pays to take the initiative wherever and whenever possible. Don't get tied down with pointless details and make sure that everyone knows you are up for a challenge. You have what it takes to win out in sporting activities, though you would be wise to take extra care. It's the best way to avoid strains and sprains.

23 SATURDAY *Moon Age Day 15   Moon Sign Aries*

Be open to new and enlightening experiences during this most positive spell in your life. Anything that widens your horizons is favourable, whilst sitting and watching life go by is not to be recommended at this time. You can best avoid family arguments by refusing to become involved. On the contrary, you now have the ability to settle disputes.

24 SUNDAY *Moon Age Day 16   Moon Sign Taurus*

Travel offers you opportunities to broaden your mind further, and is not simply a means for personal enjoyment at this time. It doesn't matter whether the journeys you are making are long or short. The important factor is that you are willing to shake up your life and to do things that under normal circumstances you might avoid.

25 MONDAY
Moon Age Day 17   Moon Sign Taurus

There are signs that in discussions or conversations you might now be prone to emotional irritations. This may be linked to your expectations of what others should or shouldn't be saying. The result is a little confusion about what it is you really want from those closest to you. Why not spend some time alone and think things through?

26 TUESDAY
Moon Age Day 18   Moon Sign Gemini

You can now ensure that family relationships are be happy and fulfilling for most of the time. The Moon is in your solar fourth house, encouraging you to turn your mind in the direction of your home, and dissuading you from wandering about quite as much. Personal attachments hold the key to finding the greatest happiness of all now.

27 WEDNESDAY
Moon Age Day 19   Moon Sign Gemini

Travel is the order of the day if it is possible. The need to get out and about is emphasised throughout all of this month, and shouldn't diminish at all. On the contrary, there are more and more reasons than ever to seek fresh fields and pastures new. When you are not on the move yourself, it pays to communicate with people who are.

28 THURSDAY
Moon Age Day 20   Moon Sign Cancer

Make the most of chances to achieve newer and better improvements around your home. It's natural for Pisces to want to dig in ahead of the forthcoming winter, and even if you are still looking out at the world too, you do need to feel secure at home. It's time to put plans in place that will add comfort in the weeks and months ahead.

29 FRIDAY
Moon Age Day 21   Moon Sign Cancer

Trends support a feeling of uncertainty towards specific people today. On the one hand you instinctively like them, but on the other you recognise that they might be rogues. As long as you are aware of the possible problems, any sort of relationship is fine. The difficulties only start when you don't realise what it is you are taking on.

30 SATURDAY *Moon Age Day 22   Moon Sign Cancer*

You can certainly get things worked out at a practical level today, though probably not without a significant struggle in some instances. If people don't seem too accommodating, you need to ask yourself whether it is you who is being inflexible. A little more give and take all round might help. Avoid pointless discussions or arguments.

31 SUNDAY *Moon Age Day 23   Moon Sign Leo*

Once again, long-distance travel and intellectual pursuits are well accented at present. The Sun is now in your solar ninth house – a potent position for thinking Pisces. Today is about not taking anything for granted, and about making sure you can see the winning post not far ahead, even if there is still much to be done in some directions.

November 2010

1 MONDAY
Moon Age Day 24   Moon Sign Leo

On the first day of November you need to be very sure of what you want and to work out well in advance how you are going to get it. Trying to force issues probably won't work, and psychology is your present key to success when dealing with other people. You can be quite diplomatic in your present approaches and that alone can work wonders.

2 TUESDAY
Moon Age Day 25   Moon Sign Virgo

You are now entering a fairly low-key phase and one during which you may decide to withdraw from situations that need extra energy or determination. Think of this as a time for pondering and for getting some rest. The more you try to pit yourself against situations whilst the lunar low is around, the more difficult things could become.

3 WEDNESDAY
Moon Age Day 26   Moon Sign Virgo

Don't be too demanding of yourself or others and all should go well today. It pays to sit and watch the river of life flowing for a while before you decide the time is right to jump in. For many Pisces subjects today can come as a welcome relief from certain pressures that you now recognise you have been imposing upon yourself.

4 THURSDAY
Moon Age Day 27   Moon Sign Libra

Why not opt for a change of scenery and routine if it proves at all possible to do so? Let your intuition guide you whenever circumstances allow and only turn on the more practical side of your nature when there is something concrete and immediate to be done. You now have what it takes to see well ahead of yourself in a financial sense.

YOUR DAILY GUIDE TO NOVEMBER 2010

5 FRIDAY
Moon Age Day 28   Moon Sign Libra

There are signs that your career might now become especially challenging, but probably quite interesting too. You can afford to take chances and should be less inclined to back situations only because you understand them well. It's time to get others to take notice of your opinions, and to positively shine in social situations.

6 SATURDAY
Moon Age Day 0   Moon Sign Scorpio

Your desire to broaden your horizons has probably not diminished across the last three or four weeks, and you now have scope to show it quite plainly. Bear in mind the effect your restlessness might have on those closest to you. If you explain yourself you should be able to take them with you on any journey you take, whether mental or physical.

7 SUNDAY
Moon Age Day 1   Moon Sign Scorpio

You can now press ahead with long-term ambitions, though some of these might have to be modified in the light of information that is coming in all the time. Rather than sticking to a particular way of doing things, it's worth varying your methods until you find out what works best. With everything to play for, you have a very positive time ahead of you.

8 MONDAY
Moon Age Day 2   Moon Sign Sagittarius

Life may well offer a few distractions at this time and so keeping your attention on what is going to matter in the future might not be very easy. All the same, you can find opportunities to have a good time, and social trends are especially well starred. An ideal day to bring to an end any chore that has been plaguing you for a while.

9 TUESDAY
Moon Age Day 3   Moon Sign Sagittarius

Intimate relations are highly favoured under present influences, and if you have been thinking about starting a new and deep attachment, this could be the time. Those Pisces subjects who are settled in their love lives can still take advantage of new incentives and the chance to intensify things. It pays to look after the pennies today.

10 WEDNESDAY *Moon Age Day 4 Moon Sign Capricorn*

Friendships can offer scope for rewards, and you should be able to make progress when you are dealing with colleagues. There is much to be said for focusing plenty of attention on work today. If you are retired or between jobs at present, one option is to put some effort into the community in some way. New interests are available now.

11 THURSDAY *Moon Age Day 5 Moon Sign Capricorn*

It may seem as if you don't have to make too much effort in order to get your professional life on an even keel. On the contrary, it could appear that things are falling into place of their own accord, and long-range ambitions look especially well starred under present trends. Support for younger relatives can make all the difference now.

12 FRIDAY *Moon Age Day 6 Moon Sign Capricorn*

You will need to get over certain hurdles if you are going to get quite as much from your social life as you would wish. Not everyone around you might be equally easy to deal with at this time, and it's worth being somewhat diplomatic. Fortunately diplomacy is your middle name, and you can also talk your way into or out of any situation.

13 SATURDAY *Moon Age Day 7 Moon Sign Aquarius*

Be prepared to deal with small setbacks today and tomorrow. These are linked to the position of the Moon in your solar twelfth house, which supports a quieter and less reactive interlude than has been evident recently. Extra effort might be required, and there's nothing wrong with withdrawing if your energy levels are depleted.

14 SUNDAY *Moon Age Day 8 Moon Sign Aquarius*

You would be wise to keep it fairly steady for today, though you still have scope to achieve some material progress. There are signs that some Pisces subjects could think they are sickening for something or other, though this probably isn't the case. By tomorrow a sudden burst of energy will assist you to get back to the centre of things.

15 MONDAY *Moon Age Day 9   Moon Sign Pisces*

The lunar high gives you everything you need to get on and to take steps in the direction of personal achievement. You need to capitalise on the newer and better incentives that Lady Luck now offers you. Any distractions you have to deal with needn't prevent you from doing anything you wish. A day to keep up the social pressure.

16 TUESDAY *Moon Age Day 10   Moon Sign Pisces*

It's time to use your Midas touch when it comes to financial matters. You have what it takes to get things to fall into place for you, and there are gains to be made that you probably didn't expect at all. What really sets today apart is your ability to latch on to opportunities at the drop of a hat and to run with them. Altogether a favourable day.

17 WEDNESDAY *Moon Age Day 11   Moon Sign Aries*

When it comes to organising things at a practical level you should be second to none at this time. Your ability to pursue monetary gains is still emphasised, and even though the lunar high is now out of the way the positive incentives remain present. Why not go out and look for a bargain today, perhaps in the company of friends?

18 THURSDAY *Moon Age Day 12   Moon Sign Aries*

Today works best if you are intuitive and willing to listen to your famous spiritual inspiration. You are in a position to keep life both busy and eventful, but also exciting and generally happy. When it comes to social trends, don't be afraid to confront completely new situations and environments. Allow yourself to be wisely led now.

19 FRIDAY *Moon Age Day 13   Moon Sign Aries*

Be prepared to give aspects of your personal life a little more support today, and to seek the sort of contentment in a personal sense that sometimes eludes you. Beware of just doing things without thinking, because there is a possibility that you could get out of your depth in some situations. Asking for extra help could well be the key.

YOUR DAILY GUIDE TO NOVEMBER 2010

20 SATURDAY *Moon Age Day 14   Moon Sign Taurus*

Long-term ambitions can be given a useful boost, and there is much to be said for going with the flow in professional matters. It's important to avoid conflict if you can this weekend, and to make the best of a fairly mixed bag, with the focus on both domestic and friendship situations. This can be a positive day for activity.

21 SUNDAY *Moon Age Day 15   Moon Sign Taurus*

You can't escape entirely from onerous duties, and these might prove to be a part of your Sunday. Your best approach is to intersperse them with happier and more enjoyable possibilities. It pays to seek support from friends at this time, and this would be an ideal time to mix freely with people who have been on the edge of your life.

22 MONDAY *Moon Age Day 16   Moon Sign Gemini*

It's natural at this time to have feelings of nostalgia relating to specific situations of a domestic and personal nature. Maybe you have been getting out the family snapshots or thinking about events for which anniversaries are due. All of this is fine, but what really counts at the moment is pushing yourself solidly towards the future.

23 TUESDAY *Moon Age Day 17   Moon Sign Gemini*

You can take advantage of boundless energy at the moment, and this is linked to the Sun, which today has moved into your solar tenth house. This would be a favourable time to take a step up the professional ladder and to investigate openings that you are only now seeing for the first time. For some Pisceans a change of job isn't out of the question.

24 WEDNESDAY *Moon Age Day 18   Moon Sign Gemini*

You are now in a position to make good things happen, even when you least expect them to do so. Pick up on this natural good fortune and run with it. Pisces is sometimes a little slow to take advantage of things, but with the Sun in its present position you have the impetus to react. Enjoy the love you can attract from others.

YOUR DAILY GUIDE TO NOVEMBER 2010

25 THURSDAY   *Moon Age Day 19   Moon Sign Cancer*

You are best suited at this time to being where the action is. Although yours is not the most outgoing or dynamic sign of the zodiac, when things do begin to work out well for you it is possible for you to ride the wave. With everything to play for in a professional sense, you could be making gains as a result of someone's misfortune.

26 FRIDAY   *Moon Age Day 20   Moon Sign Cancer*

Career and general professional trends look positive, and you have cards to play that will put you in a favourable position. Most important of all is your ability to stay in the good books of others, and you need to remember that people could be watching you closely. If not everyone seems to like you at this time, is it down to envy on their part?

27 SATURDAY   *Moon Age Day 21   Moon Sign Leo*

Your effectiveness in a general sense could be seen as exceptional. This might be especially true at work, though of course you may not even be at work on a Saturday. The weekend has plenty to offer in a social and personal sense, and all the supportive trends that surround you at present offer scope for both personal and professional rewards.

28 SUNDAY   *Moon Age Day 22   Moon Sign Leo*

An important issue could remind you of your limitations and may bring you up with a bump. Ask yourself whether this is as a result of something you have forgotten, which might not be surprising if you are very busy. Confidence remains generally high, and there are only small situations that might find you slightly unsure of things.

29 MONDAY   *Moon Age Day 23   Moon Sign Virgo*

Right now you would be wise to suspend all decision-making and allow things to slow down for a couple of days. The lunar low will do you no tangible harm, though it supports an interlude of withdrawal when you may feel less confident and more doubtful about your own abilities. Be prepared to listen to friends today.

30 TUESDAY

Moon Age Day 24   Moon Sign Virgo

This is a wind-down period and a time that responds to resting. All the more reason to let others do some of the hard work whilst you monitor what is going on. Planning is just as important as doing and in this sense the slowdown offered by the lunar low can be a friend. You needn't be too quick to take offence over something relatively unimportant.

December 2010

1 WEDNESDAY — *Moon Age Day 25   Moon Sign Libra*

Today your intuition should be right on the ball. This is partly assisted by the present position of the Moon, and if you use this influence to the full you could easily shock yourself and everyone around you! There's nothing wrong with being forthright when it comes to expressing your feelings, though it's unusual for diplomatic Pisces.

2 THURSDAY — *Moon Age Day 26   Moon Sign Libra*

Don't push too hard in a material sense and allow certain situations to mature. All good recipes need to cook steadily and you need to apply this in your life just now. Leaving things alone will give you more time to concentrate on your personal and social life, both of which are well accented under present trends.

3 FRIDAY — *Moon Age Day 27   Moon Sign Scorpio*

Now is the time to identify new openings and opportunities that you might have missed during a very busy November. The nuances of life are more evident and you needn't be at all reticent to take steps you would have avoided even a few weeks ago. Renewed confidence regarding an old issue might encourage you to start something again.

4 SATURDAY — *Moon Age Day 28   Moon Sign Scorpio*

You could now register a little pressure, possibly from the direction of colleagues or, in some specific situations, from friends. On a different tack you have an opportunity to get your love life running very smoothly, and with the festive season in your sights you might already be getting quite romantic and gooey about Christmas time.

YOUR DAILY GUIDE TO DECEMBER 2010

5 SUNDAY *Moon Age Day 29   Moon Sign Sagittarius*

Trends today emphasise your strong need to excel in some way. This might not be too easy on a Sunday, and you may decide to use this as a chance to plan something very carefully for later in the week. In the meantime, it's worth getting together with those you care for and making plans that are going to be necessary for later in the month.

6 MONDAY *Moon Age Day 0   Moon Sign Sagittarius*

Venus is now in your solar ninth house and this planetary position encourages you to spread your wings. It's a question of trying something new at every possible opportunity and doing what you can to free yourself from irksome responsibilities. If friends have good ideas at the moment, see whether any of these appeal to you.

7 TUESDAY *Moon Age Day 1   Moon Sign Capricorn*

You have a talent for making friends and can really show this at the moment. By all means welcome plenty of people into your life, and whilst you can't make all of them bosom buddies you should be happy to oblige as many of them as you can. When it comes to making financial gains the key is to be in the right place at the best possible time.

8 WEDNESDAY *Moon Age Day 2   Moon Sign Capricorn*

Today's trends favour mental interests and you can afford to stretch yourself in all sorts of ways. Be prepared to look at the sort of travel that can broaden your horizons and to consider visiting places of educational interest. Passing on something you know about is also par for the course on a day when you may be interacting all the time.

9 THURSDAY *Moon Age Day 3   Moon Sign Capricorn*

There are signs that your dogmatic attitude might cause disagreements today, and you may be rather too sure of yourself for once. This is quite unusual for Pisces, but of course there are times for all of us when we are certain of what we are saying. The more diplomatic you manage to be the better, but some clashes could be inevitable.

10 FRIDAY *Moon Age Day 4   Moon Sign Aquarius*

As the Moon moves into your solar twelfth house a slight lull in proceedings would be no bad thing. It might seem as if your power to make things happen has been withdrawn, but this should only be a very temporary state of affairs. As a result, today is better for planning than for doing, and there is much to be said for enlisting help.

11 SATURDAY ☿ *Moon Age Day 5   Moon Sign Aquarius*

You can use your social network to bring you through your quieter moments now, and needn't shy away from involvement in the schemes of others. Rather than making important moves today, why not wait until tomorrow? It's time to clear the decks for action in a practical sense and to prepare yourself for the lunar high that is coming.

12 SUNDAY ☿ *Moon Age Day 6   Moon Sign Pisces*

The lunar high urges you to press ahead in order to get what you want. This is a Sunday, and as a result some things won't be possible, especially in a professional sense, but you have what it takes to get ahead. From a social point of view your star is in the ascendant, and this assists you to show others the most likeable side of your nature.

13 MONDAY ☿ *Moon Age Day 7   Moon Sign Pisces*

Put new plans and schemes into action right now! You need to start this working week as you mean to go on, and there is every reason to believe that the planets can help you at each new twist and turn. Keep focused on new initiatives and don't give opponents the chance to get one over on you. It's just a case of paying attention.

14 TUESDAY ☿ *Moon Age Day 8   Moon Sign Pisces*

Getting involved with life at a hands-on level offers you the best chance of making progress. This could even be of a financial as well as a practical sort. Make the most of the natural good luck that is available during the lunar high and also be sure that everyone knows you are around. Plan now for Christmas parties and outings.

YOUR DAILY GUIDE TO DECEMBER 2010

15 WEDNESDAY ☿   *Moon Age Day 9   Moon Sign Aries*

This should be an optimistic period and one in which you can pursue advancement and greater recognition in your professional life. Bear in mind that various people could be paying attention to your activities, so it pays to make sure you remain in the spotlight. Confidence remains emphasised, though emotions might be shaky.

16 THURSDAY ☿   *Moon Age Day 10   Moon Sign Aries*

Any way that you can make more of your natural talents is worth following. Your strength lies in your willingness to broaden your horizons and to seek out new material that gives you a better understanding of life. This process never stops for Pisces and has nothing to do with age. By all means continue to welcome newcomers into your life.

17 FRIDAY ☿   *Moon Age Day 11   Moon Sign Taurus*

Today's major sources of joy and pleasure include friends and colleagues, particularly those who are especially attractive and approachable around now. Pisces people should certainly be casting their minds ahead and towards Christmas, and it's natural to get excited about the special things you have planned.

18 SATURDAY ☿   *Moon Age Day 12   Moon Sign Taurus*

Capitalise today on what you hear from other people. It is certainly worth keeping your ears open, because even the most inconsequential conversations can give you good ideas. The more you mix and mingle with different sorts of people, the greater is your chance of achieving something that has been important to you for ages.

19 SUNDAY ☿   *Moon Age Day 13   Moon Sign Taurus*

Trends suggest that you function at your best right now when there is peace and harmony at home. For this reason alone you would be wise to avoid getting involved in family rows, and at the same time nip any disputes between other family members in the bud. Keeping people happy might be as simple as giving them something to do.

YOUR DAILY GUIDE TO DECEMBER 2010

20 MONDAY ☿ *Moon Age Day 14   Moon Sign Gemini*

You should make the most of opportunities to do what takes your fancy at this stage of the month, even if you feel slightly hedged in by responsibilities. The spotlight is on romance, and this is an ideal time to find new ways of showing your affection. Be prepared to listen carefully to what younger people have to say.

21 TUESDAY ☿ *Moon Age Day 15   Moon Sign Gemini*

Now there should be very little to upset the general forward progress you make in life. It's true that you might be rather bogged down with plans for the holidays but this shouldn't bother you in the slightest because most Pisceans love Christmas. If you can't move about too much physically at the moment, you can at least dream in a big way.

22 WEDNESDAY ☿ *Moon Age Day 16   Moon Sign Cancer*

You should now function best when you are in team situations or when you take advantage of social invitations. Concentrating on solo activities might not be quite so fortunate under present trends, which is why you need to be associating with others all the time. Stand by to make the most of surprises, and maybe even a present you will treasure.

23 THURSDAY ☿ *Moon Age Day 17   Moon Sign Cancer*

When it comes to social situations you can afford to assert yourself rather strongly at the moment. This helps you to make sure you are not an 'also-ran' in any situation. On the contrary, it's a question of being out there in the lead and making the rules. Be ready for some excitement at home, especially amongst younger family members.

24 FRIDAY ☿ *Moon Age Day 18   Moon Sign Leo*

Your ability to work hard and with great intensity is highlighted, but at the same time there may be distractions that have nothing to do with practical or professional matters. By this evening you should be ready to lay down the traces of responsibility and to give yourself fully to all the magic and romance you can create at this time of year.

YOUR DAILY GUIDE TO DECEMBER 2010

25 SATURDAY ☿ *Moon Age Day 19   Moon Sign Leo*

Travel and exploration of all kinds could well appeal to you, even though this is Christmas Day and you might be expected to play the dutiful host. If you do get the chance to get out, it's worth doing things that stimulate your mind and that add to your store of social contacts. Your generosity can make all the difference at the moment.

26 SUNDAY ☿ *Moon Age Day 20   Moon Sign Virgo*

A slower Boxing Day is possible because the lunar low is around. In some ways this might be a good thing because it encourages you to stay closer to home and could help you to curb some of the restless tendencies that surround you under present planetary trends. You might even decide to sit and watch television!

27 MONDAY ☿ *Moon Age Day 21   Moon Sign Virgo*

Life in a general sense can prove to be slightly taxing, but as long as you are not pushing yourself too hard you may not even notice the restrictions that are present. Let others take some of the strain in terms of all arrangements at home.

28 TUESDAY ☿ *Moon Age Day 22   Moon Sign Libra*

The lunar low is now out of the way and almost immediately you can thrust yourself into the mainstream of activity. This is an ideal time to take the lead in any situation, and to recognise that people may be relying on you to a much greater extent.

29 WEDNESDAY ☿ *Moon Age Day 23   Moon Sign Libra*

There are signs today that you may have to deal with disputes and arguments, none of which have anything directly to do with you. Your best response is to stay neutral and don't even get involved as an honest broker. Let other people sort things out.

30 THURSDAY ☿ *Moon Age Day 24   Moon Sign Scorpio*

This is a time for serious thinking and maybe for casting your mind forward towards a new year. At the same time you need to keep your thinking light and airy and don't get bogged down with irrelevant details. The honesty of friends is emphasised.

31 FRIDAY *Moon Age Day 25   Moon Sign Scorpio*

Most co-operative discussions can be steered in your direction, and you are in a position to impress others with your efforts on their behalf. By this evening you should be ready to party and to contribute to a happy time.

RISING SIGNS FOR PISCES

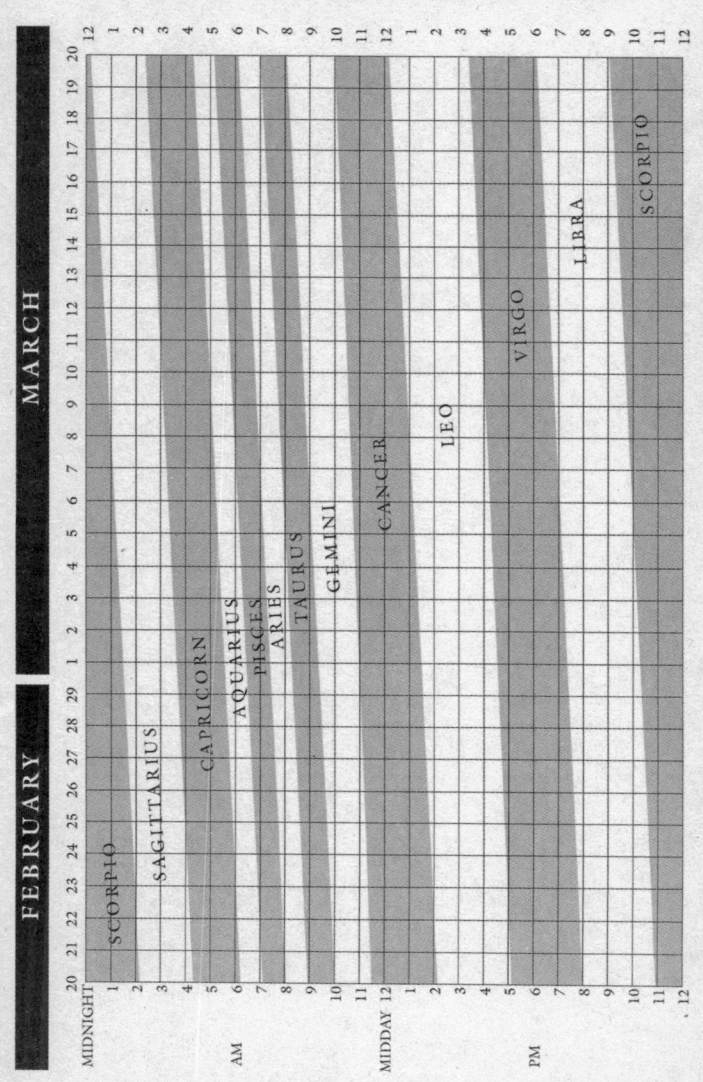

THE ZODIAC, PLANETS AND CORRESPONDENCES

The Earth revolves around the Sun once every calendar year, so when viewed from Earth the Sun appears in a different part of the sky as the year progresses. In astrology, these parts of the sky are divided into the signs of the zodiac and this means that the signs are organised in a circle. The circle begins with Aries and ends with Pisces.

Taking the zodiac sign as a starting point, astrologers then work with all the positions of planets, stars and many other factors to calculate horoscopes and birth charts and tell us what the stars have in store for us.

The table below shows the planets and Elements for each of the signs of the zodiac. Each sign belongs to one of the four Elements: Fire, Air, Earth or Water. Fire signs are creative and enthusiastic; Air signs are mentally active and thoughtful; Earth signs are constructive and practical; Water signs are emotional and have strong feelings.

It also shows the metals and gemstones associated with, or corresponding with, each sign. The correspondence is made when a metal or stone possesses properties that are held in common with a particular sign of the zodiac.

Finally, the table shows the opposite of each star sign – this is the opposite sign in the astrological circle.

Placed	Sign	Symbol	Element	Planet	Metal	Stone	Opposite
1	Aries	Ram	Fire	Mars	Iron	Bloodstone	Libra
2	Taurus	Bull	Earth	Venus	Copper	Sapphire	Scorpio
3	Gemini	Twins	Air	Mercury	Mercury	Tiger's Eye	Sagittarius
4	Cancer	Crab	Water	Moon	Silver	Pearl	Capricorn
5	Leo	Lion	Fire	Sun	Gold	Ruby	Aquarius
6	Virgo	Maiden	Earth	Mercury	Mercury	Sardonyx	Pisces
7	Libra	Scales	Air	Venus	Copper	Sapphire	Aries
8	Scorpio	Scorpion	Water	Pluto	Plutonium	Jasper	Taurus
9	Sagittarius	Archer	Fire	Jupiter	Tin	Topaz	Gemini
10	Capricorn	Goat	Earth	Saturn	Lead	Black Onyx	Cancer
11	Aquarius	Waterbearer	Air	Uranus	Uranium	Amethyst	Leo
12	Pisces	Fishes	Water	Neptune	Tin	Moonstone	Virgo